R/C DUCTED FANS

HOW TO BUILD AND FLY YOUR OWN JET SUCCESSFULLY

Frank Fanelli

Motorbooks International
Publishers & Wholesalers Inc.
Osceola, Wisconsin 54020, USA ®

First published in 1987 by Motorbooks International Publishers & Wholesalers Inc., PO Box 2, 729 Prospect Avenue, Osceola, WI 54020 USA

Printed and bound in the United States of America

Library of Congress Cataloging-in-Publication Data
Fanelli, Frank.
    R/C ducted fans.

    Includes index.
    1. Airplanes—Models—Motors.   2. Turbofan engines.
I. Title   II. Title: RC ducted fans.
RL777.F36   1987   626.133'134   87-28105
ISBN 0-87938-279-1 (soft)

Cover photo taken by Frank Fanelli: veteran ducted-fan modeler Mike Kulczyk's magnificent model of a Saab AJ37 Viggen, intimately detailed from the cockpit to the revolutionary ducted-fan power. Line drawings by Scott Lengle.

Contents

Foreword

Much has been written about ducted fans, most of it highly technical, precious little of it practical. The technical material is certainly helpful for the modeler who chooses to design his own airframe, and so this volume addresses the key issues of design for those who require it. More importantly, however, is the fact that the primary purpose of what you are about to read is to present material which captures the overall ducted-fan scene in understandable terms, essential to the newcomer while still interesting to the accomplished fan enthusiast.

Three basic points which should be kept in mind as you fly your way through this book are:

1. All ducted fans work, quite literally, as air pumps. Air is drawn in through an inlet, accelerated by the fan rotor (propeller) and ejected through an outlet, generally a tailpipe, creating thrust.

2. Presently available fan units are designed for specific power range engines. Therefore, the "hottest" engine will spin the rotor at the highest rpm, producing the most static thrust. I know of no recommended engine fan combination that will allow the fan rotor to overspeed or stall, decreasing thrust.

3. You don't have to be an engine wizard to successfully operate a ducted-fan airplane. The engine-fan systems manufacturers are providing powerful, reliable, matched components that allow the use of sport (five to ten percent nitro) fuels and still provide more than adequate power.

Ducted-fan propulsion systems are not new. Much of the early work was done in Britain by P. E. Norman with his work being carried on even today by his son, Marcus.

Some of the modelers on this side of the Atlantic, a number of which you'll hear mentioned throughout this book such as Mike Kulczyk, Bill Effinger and Bob Kress, had the wheels in motion nearly thirty years ago. What they achieved, especially considering the resources available, is truly an accomplishment! Power-limited engines, aluminum or mica hand-formed rotors and delicate airframes were the order of the day. Most of these adventures were free-flight models and performed marginally—but they did fly, paving the way for the present breed of fans.

Today's ultra-small, high-reliability radios, incredibly powerful engines and computer-designed fan units and airframes have opened up a whole new world . . . only the surface of which has yet to be scratched.

Rich Uravitch

Preface

Ducted-fan models have arrived. These fascinating aircraft are now ready to enter the mainstream of modeling with a consistent reliability, an acceptable level of building ease and surprisingly stable flight characteristics. While there still are no fan models for the raw beginner or novice, there are now kits and plans for the performance fanatic to the average Sunday flier.

The learning curve required to successfully enter the field has been flattened thanks to the persistent efforts of some dedicated fan modelers who wanted to bring the jet age to modeling. Their sometimes remarkable achievements cost years of frustration and determination. This book documents those achievements and outlines the difficulties they faced because they serve as a perfect introduction to fan modeling. It is a book to encourage anyone who wants to get involved with fans to go ahead and do it.

What you read here comes from the best in the fan field, as one thing characterizes all of them: their willingness to patiently answer questions and help other modelers learn. Many of the people you read about here indirectly wrote this book with the information they generously provided. Tom Cook of Jet Model Products, Bob Kress of Kress Jets, Marc Jensen of Byron Originals, Mike Kulczyk of Flying Models and Bob Violett of Bob Violett Models all endured many phone calls, generously provided materials and critiqued the rough draft of this book

"Jet Blast" columnist Rich Uravitch, however, deserves special mention and thanks. From the first time I started to cover ducted fans for *Flying Models* magazine, he has continued to offer not only help but encouragement that transcends any rivalry.

There's something for anyone who loves jets. If you like to tinker with the exotic, puncture the sound barrier, or simply drool over the fluid grace of jets, ducted fans are for you. Join the jet age.

Frank Fanelli

Chapter 1

History and development

Ducted-fan aircraft systems have blossomed since modelers began experimenting with them in the mid-1950s. The refined and reliable modern powerplants have opened up the realm of scale jet and sport jet aircraft to dedicated scale craftsmen and experienced sport fliers. With the development of new versatile materials and stronger airframes, ducted-fan jet modeling is one of the revolutionary fields of radio control flying.

The ducted-fan unit is not a true jet engine which uses heat to compress air for thrust. Instead, a ducted fan is a refined multibladed propeller running inside a duct to achieve better thrust efficiency. The essential requirements of any model fan system are a multibladed impeller, a shroud, an engine mount and airflow straighteners, called stators.

Ducted fans are not new. In the aviation world, a similar propulsion system was used as early as 1938 in the Italian Caproni-Campini N.1. In the 1950s English and American modelers began experimenting with various forms of ducted-fan units in free flight and control-line planes. Yet modelers who pursued this field of the hobby—especially control-line and R/C—were confined by material and powerplant shortcomings. There were plenty of

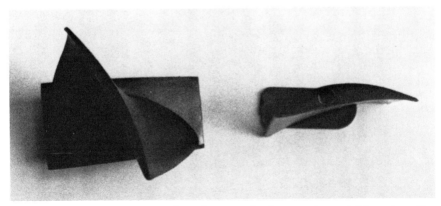

This picture shows the relationship of impeller blade, left, and stator blade, *right. Stator takes swirl from impeller and straightens the flow.*

conventional piston-powered subjects which could be modeled with more ease.

To put into perspective the problems facing the ducted-fan modeler in the fifties consider that there were no glass fiber resins in use in the hobby at that time, the standard material for fan impellers today. Fiberglass technology, so useful in providing strong, light airframes of the complex geometric shapes found in scale jet aircraft, was still in its infancy. Powerplants were limited by weaker alloys and inferior porting, and could not provide the horsepower or the high rpm which make the modern fans practical. After all, the full-size jet engine was still in its own adolescence.

The dedicated pioneer jet modelers then had two choices. They could use the Dynajet, an unthrottled pulse jet with adequate thrust, or they could experiment and improvise their own systems—fans in cans, as they were affectionately known.

The Dynajet was impractical. Besides possessing an all-or-nothing thrust, the unit required compressed air to trigger it. Starting was a complex procedure, and the exhaust had to be shielded so it would not set the model on fire. This powerful, impractical unit later found its niche in a specialized form of control-line racing.

This left modelers with ducted fans as the one choice for jet models without external props, as there were no true turbine powerplants that could be used. The fan units, jury-rigged by today's standards, worked even

One of Mike Kulczyk's early home-made fans in a can. The shroud is a simple tin can; the impeller is made of wood blades. Mike Kulczyk

with the relatively low-powered glow engines of the time. Airframes had to be extraordinarily light.

To achieve the desired thrust, it was established early on that specific factors were involved in the fan system. First, the number of blades on the impeller was important. Second, the pitch of these blades worked in relation to both the number of blades and the impeller's diameter. Third, the contraction of the tailpipe played an important part in the efficiency of the thrust generated.

The resulting fans in cans were just that—multibladed, small-diameter propellers inside coffee cans or other suitable ducts in the airframe. The impeller (the terms impeller, rotor or fan are interchangeable) was made in a variety of ways. Some consisted of a hardwood hub with diagonal slots cut in it to bed the individual fan blades. These fan blades were thin plywood or, in some cases, thin rigid sheet metal or aluminum. Most were flat, without camber. Some modelers used a flat circular sheet of thin rigid metal with each blade section cut and carefully bent to shape, forming a single-piece impeller. Other modelers experimented with curved blades,

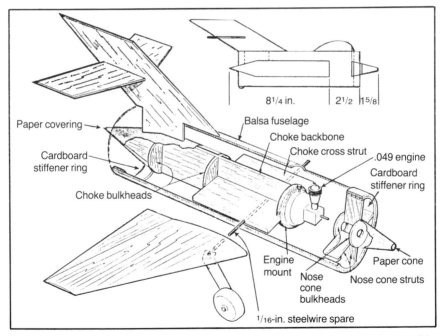

This shows a 1954 vintage C/L ducted-fan plane which used a homebrew fan in a small airframe. It's called the Jaunty Alouette and was designed by American fan pioneer Roy Clough.

As an economic way of producing impellers, some modelers tried stamped
and pressed sheet metal impellers.
They fatigued easily at high rpm and
thus were impractical.

This is an early experimental impeller
with a wood hub. Angled slots have
been milled in the hub to accept the ten
aluminum impeller blades.

Here is shown a variety of commercial
and homemade impellers. Of all these
impellers, only the Boss 602 impeller,

bottom center, and the Byro-Jet impeller, middle row, right, have survived.

much harder to make and according to some, less efficient. Later fans used aluminum hubs with the blade slots milled out individually. All of these fans were simply attached to the front of a suitable glow engine and then mounted inside some sort of duct. The duct material could be a tin can or, if a suitable diameter could not be found, a thin 1/64 plywood duct.

The number of blades on a fan varied. Some tried up to sixteen blades per fan, but six blades seemed the most effective for matching the peak brake horsepower of the engines available. One program's test results indicated that the increased solidity (the total amount of blade area in relation to the swept area of all the blades) either adversely loaded the engine or, because of the decreased diameter, allowed it to overrev beyond its peak horsepower.

Experiments with the tailpipe diameters and the intake diameters established that the intake should be kept as large as possible while the tailpipe exit should be approximately ninety percent of the swept area of the fan blades, not including the hub. Early experiments also showed that as the tailpipe diameter decreased, the compression effect on the airflow inside the duct cut the efficiency of the thrust. If the tailpipe were decreased fifty percent, the impeller would stall.

The intake duct and the thrust ducts of these early models reflect the shortcomings of the materials. Often, the model's intake was simply an opening on the nose, the wing roots or the sides of the fuselage. There was no

These are some samples of homemade impellers. All except the one at the lower right corner are wood. The lower one has aluminum blades and an aluminum hub with milled blade slots. Mike Kulczyk

English ducted-fan pioneer P. E. Norman holds an early 1960s scratchbuilt MiG-15 design of his. Dick Sarpolus

11

interior ductwork leading to the fan inside because there was no material light enough to mold into the proper duct shape. The more necessary thrust duct or tube was thin cardboard, rolled and taped on a form and then coated with dope to make it fuel proof.

These early experiments defined the problems to be overcome and provided a foundation on which to build future fans. Many of these principles still hold, corroborated by present-day fan unit designs.

From the 1950s through the 1960s there were few commercial ventures regarding ducted fans. The English Veron fan was the sole unit on the market up until 1972, and it was simply an impeller. The modeler had to make his or her own duct and engine mounting.

Coverage of ducted-fan modeling has been almost nonexistent, with only a few articles documenting the progress of jet models. Probably the best known jet modeler is the late Englishman P. E. Norman, a prolific designer of airframes and ducted-fan units, primarily for radio control. The heavy radio system, the low power of the early engines and the weak homemade impellers forced him and others to pare down airframes to the least possible weight. Landing gear was usually sacrificed; Norman resorted to launching models from dollies and landing them belly-up in the grass.

In the United States, Bill Effinger, Henry Struck and Mike Kulczyk experimented with ducted fans. Effinger and Struck, associated with Berkeley Models, actually produced three scale free-flight models powered by

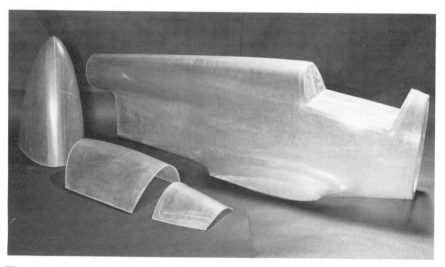

This is an illustrative fiberglass fuselage as it comes from a Byron Originals BD-5J kit. It's made of polyester resin and fiberglass cloth in six-ounce weights.

0.049 cubic inch engines with simple ducts and stamped metal impellers. The planes flew quite well.

Kulczyk started in the late 1950s to design a number of scale control-line ducted fans and continued from 1968 to design radio-control ducted fans. His first such aircraft was a control-line Saab J-35 Draken using a homemade all-metal impeller. It didn't work well, however, because the weight of the impeller acted as a gyroscope and vibration literally shook the aircraft apart. His next venture used an all-wood impeller driven by an Enya .19. The thrust level achieved was a dismal one pound, but it still flew the eighty-inch U-2 spyplane.

One of the most important events for modern-day fans was the refinement of proportional radios. Until the late 1960s the servo case dimensions, battery pack size and receiver size were serious constraints on all radio-control modelers. To the ducted-fan modeler who was further limited by a powerplant and a duct which took up most of the model's insides, radio size and weight were almost insurmountable obstacles. What limited space was available after the powerplant and radio sometimes worked against the center of gravity requirements forcing balancing weights to be added. The radios of that time were also more susceptible to interference from the use of long servo leads or metal-to-metal contacts. This prevented placing servos in remote locations such as wings for direct linkage to a control.

In the early 1970s, engine manufacturers turned their attention to developing high-power, high-rpm engines. Up to this time most production engines used cross-flow scavenging of the engine cylinder. The technique did not allow high rpm, something that fan-unit designers needed to produce a significant increase in thrust. Pylon racing engines seemed to be the only suitable powerplant, but they too had a severe limitation, being unthrottled.

The final development to launch present-day fans was the arrival of fiberglass technology for fuselage production. Model airframes up to the mid-seventies were wood, which was an excellent material, yet it limited airframes to simple shapes. For those who wanted to model more sophisticated aerodynamic shapes such as jets, wood required an involved framework and the consequent penalty in weight, something which the fan powerplants could not handle.

The J. J. Scozzifavva-Bob Violett team was the first to bring modern fans to national attention in 1972. Scozzifavva was the designer of the Scozzi, now known as the Turbax family of ducted-fan units. He was a mechanical engineer who was attracted to the idea of designing a ducted fan that would be powerful, practical and efficient. He first assessed the two-cycle glow engines and realized that the racing .40s were the only ones that could provide the high rpm and horsepower required for ducted fans.

The K&B 40S could pack an unheard-of 2 hp into an engine the size of a .40 case. To prove the concept's feasibility, Scozzifavva bought a high-performance electronics cooling fan (the type used in military aircraft), hooked up a K&B 40S, and bench ran the unit. Though crude, the results

13

Still a widely used fan model, the A-4 Skyhawk designed by Bob Violett was *highly successful with the Turbax I fan unit.*

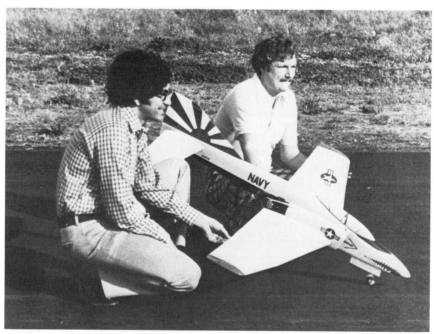

Designer of the Turbax I fan, James Scozzifavva, is on the left; the designer of the famous Sundowner, Bob Violett, is on the right. The Sundowner, which *used the original Turbax I fan, demonstrated in the early-1970s that a fan-powered plane could perform on par with pattern aircraft.*

14

encouraged him to refine the unit and have a master impeller blade design drawn up for a five-inch-diameter fan unit. The first prototype impeller was an all-aluminum machined unit with four blades. When K&B introduced the K&B 6.5 cubic centimeter engine in early 1972, Scozzifavva added a fifth blade to the impeller to make use of the extra horsepower.

Violett was a prominent R/C pylon racer. Since Scozzifavva and Violett shared the desire for performance, they agreed to test the fan unit in a high-performance design. The all-aluminum unit was mounted in a test model and flown until all the bugs were worked out. This marked the birth of the Sundowner. Violett brought the plane to the 1973 Lakehurst Pylon Championships and won the event with a top speed of 110 mph. The model had a swept delta wing with the fan unit suspended underneath. With the Scozzi fan, the blazing performance caught everyone's attention.

Violett went on to design and fly a scale model of the Douglas A-4 Skyhawk using the production version of the Scozzi fan which now incorporated the new K&B 7.5 Model 9100 fan engine. The Skyhawk, first kitted by Violett and now sold by Jet Hangar Hobbies, has remained one of the best flying and most popular ducted-fan designs. The K&B 7.5 became the staple fan engine for years to follow.

Within a few years of the Scozzifavva-Violett success, several designers finalized independent efforts with a variety of airframe and fan unit designs, all of which took advantage of the new fiberglass-resin technology and the new high-horsepower, high-rpm engines. In 1975, Bob Kress of Kress Jets began designing a series of fan units in four sizes to widen the potential use of ducted fans. His Axiflo series, which was introduced late in 1977, included the two-inch RK-049 (.049 engine), the four-inch RK-20 (.21 or 3.5 engines) and the five-inch RK-40 (.40 ci). A large six-inch fan, the RK-60 (.60 or .65 ci engine), never came into production. The shell was injected nylon, as were the impeller, stators and engine mount. The series was later refined to use glass resins.

Byron Originals, a company headed by Byron Godberson, produced in 1979 an R/C ducted-fan package for everyone with a large yet simple six-

The Axiflo 20 fan was the most successful of the Bob Kress-designed Axiflo series. It used a 3.5 cc or .21–.25 ci displacement engine.

inch fan unit powered by .61 and larger engines and a fiberglass kit of the MiG-15 as a ducted-fan trainer. The impeller and shroud of the fan unit were both injection-molded reinforced glass nylon, a material used frequently now for high-strength, high-stress applications. The unit deviated from common fan design in that it had the engine mounted in front of the fan instead of behind it. The MiG-15 kit defined the later Byron kit concept with a molded fiberglass fuselage and injection-molded foam wings and stabilizers, a process used for the first time in ducted-fan kits.

At about the same time, Tom Cook, an experienced scale modeler, began experimenting with scale jet aircraft designs. His first model was a Messerschmidt Me-262, the twin-engine World War II German fighter that became the first operational military jet. The model Me-262 used twin Scozzi fans driven by K&B 6.5 racing engines. Yet duct problems and engine sensitivity led to a number of crashes. With one engine out, the asymmetric thrust made the model virtually uncontrollable.

In an effort to find a suitable airframe to overcome the thrust problem, Cook designed a large twin-engined F-4D Phantom with two Scozzi fans. The plane first appeared at the 1980 Scale Masters tournament, and its impressive size and performance showed that larger, complex-shaped jet aircraft could be successfully modeled with the ducted-fan powerplants then available.

Just prior to Cook's success, Larry Wolfe began Jet Hangar Hobbies. His company provided several excellent airframes for the Scozzi fan, now

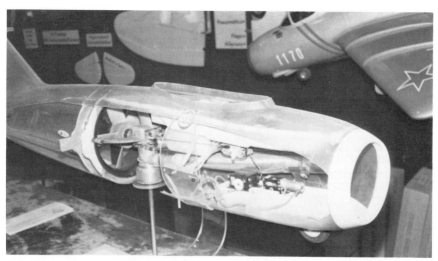

Cutaway model shows the internal arrangement of the Byron Originals MiG-15, the first fan model to use the

Byro-Jet. Finished model is in background.

The Byron Originals MiG 15 was their first ducted-fan plane, also the first to use the Byro-Jet fan unit. Plane makes an excellent ducted-fan trainer, as it is very stable and durable.

Tom Cook's large twin-engine Phantom attracts attention because of its size, success and appeal. Cook is shown with his son here.

This F9F-8 Cougar is one of the highly successful fan kits marketed by Jet Hangar Hobbies. The plane is designed around the Turbax I or III fan, or with minor modification, any of the five-inch rail-mount fans.

The engine that powered the Byro-Jet to top performance was the Rossi .81. Recently discontinued, it gave the Byro-Jet more than adequate thrust.

The impellers shown on the motor are an unsuccessful experimental configuration.

marketed by Jet Hangar as the Turbax fan. These airframes, Violett's A-4 Skyhawk, an F-9F Cougar and a Dassault Mirage III, provided a fiberglass fuselage and built-up wooden wings which were used to reduce weight. With the introduction of the first true ducted-fan engine, the powerful K&B 7.5 in 1979, these airframes aided many modelers getting into ducted-fan radio-control aircraft. Two of the three designs, the Skyhawk and the Mirage III, are adaptable to new fan packages and provide excellent performance.

By 1981 the fan units had standardized to three nominal sizes, the six-inch Byron, the five-inch Turbax I and the four-inch Axiflo or RK-20. Still,

First to pack more horsepower in a fan unit was the RK-740. It was slightly smaller than the older Axiflo 20 (which used a .20 ci engine) but housed a .45 ci engine driving a seven- instead of five-bladed fan. Early models were difficult to assembly because of the sheet metal shroud.

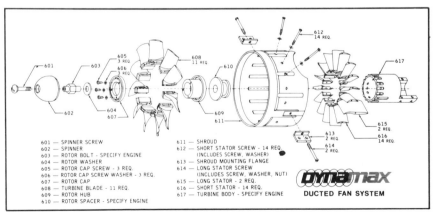

601 — SPINNER SCREW
602 — SPINNER
603 — ROTOR BOLT - SPECIFY ENGINE
604 — ROTOR WASHER
605 — ROTOR CAP SCREW - 3 REQ.
606 — ROTOR CAP SCREW WASHER - 3 REQ.
607 — ROTOR CAP
608 — TURBINE BLADE - 11 REQ.
609 — ROTOR HUB
610 — ROTOR SPACER - SPECIFY ENGINE

611 — SHROUD
612 — SHORT STATOR SCREW - 14 REQ.
    (INCLUDES SCREW, WASHER)
613 — SHROUD MOUNTING FLANGE
614 — LONG STATOR SCREW
    (INCLUDES SCREW, WASHER, NUT)
615 — LONG STATOR - 2 REQ.
616 — SHORT STATOR - 14 REQ.
617 — TURBINE BODY - SPECIFY ENGINE

DYNAMAX
DUCTED FAN SYSTEM

The schematic drawing of the Dynamax fan system can substitute as a generic illustration of any ducted fan unit.

Byron Originals' most popular kit, the
F-16, is both an excellent trainer and
flyer. It can be built either with or without retractable landing gear.

A Byron Kfir powered by a single jet.
While the canards are fashionable in
current airplane design, they are not
functioning on this model. The elevon
control requires a mixer.

there was really only one suitable engine on the market, the K&B 7.5, designed specifically for the power a fan unit needs: high horsepower through high rpm. The K&B was suited only for the five-inch Turbax and produced approximately 5 lb. of thrust. The Byron unit used a number of .61 ci pattern engines but could not achieve its capable thrust. The Axiflo used .21 engines which also failed to provide the necessary power. The design knowledge for fan units to yield even greater thrust in the same size packages was there; the engines were not.

The major step to give fan modelers more than sufficient performance was the introduction of engines designed specifically for ducted fans. Borrowing technology from high-revving marine racing engines, manufacturers developed ducted-fan engines. The Rossi .81, the Rossi .65, the O.S. Max .46 VR-DF and the O.S. Max .25 VF-DF gave all of the fan units more potent thrust. The presence of these new engines also gave fan designers the proper horsepower to design new, more efficient, more powerful fan units.

Bob Kress of Kress Jets was the first to design a new generation of fan. All fans produced in the United States had only five blades on the impeller. In 1982, Kress designed the RK-740, which was a four-inch-diameter fan (the same diameter as his earlier RK-20) but with seven blades on the impeller powered by a .45 (7.5 cc) engine! It was a case of packing more horsepower into the same size shroud and using an impeller that could absorb the required horsepower and produce more thrust.

A year or so later, Jet Hangar Hobbies introduced the Turbax III which allowed a modeler to put a .61 to .65 engine in the original .45 Scozzi/Turbax. In 1984 Tom Cook introduced the Dynamax fan, a five-inch unit

Two Byron Originals, the F-20 Tigershark in the foreground, and an F-15. Both models are monsters: the F-20 *is some 7 1/2-feet long; the F-15 is nine-feet long. They weigh in at between 25 and 35 lb. each.*

21

Bob Fiorenze's famous F-4 Phantom jet with twin ducted fans and an operational drag chute in the rear for stopping the plane on landing. Fiorenze's plane was built from a Jet Model Products kit.

A highly successful design, the Uravitch-designed F-86 was a small model designed for the four-inch fan like the Axiflo 20 or the RK-740.

with eleven blades on the impeller and room for a .61 to .81 engine. In 1986 Bob Violett Models introduced the most highly refined fan unit in use today. His Viojett was a nominal five-inch fan with a special aerodynamic shroud around the engine head to cut down thrust loss due to drag. Other refinements included a preset tuned pipe length, easy access for starting and a needle valve body on the outside of the fan shroud. It also used a specially designed engine, the KBV .72 for power.

With more powerful fan units now available and modern construction techniques such as fiberglass-foam-wood composites and materials such as carbon fiber and Kevlar, kit manufacturers have begun to refine kits. Until the Jet Model Products' Starfire kit, almost every ducted-fan airplane had to rely on cheater holes to provide sufficient air for the fan to work. These large unsightly holes cut into the bottom of the fuselage were the easiest solution to airflow problems without an internal duct. About the only other solution to the problem was the slightly more complex blow-in doors. These were spring-loaded panels on the side of the fuselage just forward of the fan which would open inward as power was increased. They were first used by Rich Uravitch on his small F-86 Sabre designed for the four-inch RK-20.

Today more manufacturers are providing kits without external holes in the fuselage and with a full internal duct from inlet to exhaust. As experience is gained, manufacturers are providing better-engineered products allowing any average modeler to successfully fly ducted-fan planes.

Chapter 2

Theory of ducted fans

Efficiency becomes important in a ducted fan because of the type of thrust it produces. A propeller and a ducted fan may produce the same amount of thrust—let's say ten pounds—but it's not like comparing apples to apples. A propeller, because of its larger diameter, will take a large amount of air and quickly accelerate it to the ten pounds of thrust. A ducted fan, smaller in diameter, takes a smaller amount of air and must accelerate it to the same ten pounds of thrust. The effect is similar to using the power of a car's engine in first versus third gear to get the car moving. In first gear, the starting is quick and effortless. In third gear, the car starts moving but accelerates slower and with greater effort because it is not an efficient use of the engine's power. Thus, in a model airplane a propeller can move the craft, overcome the drag effects of a rough field and the model's own weight, and accelerate it to a flying speed quicker than an impeller.

Aeronautical engineers know that putting a shroud around a propeller, whether it is a conventional two-bladed prop or a multibladed impeller, increases its efficiency by eliminating much of the tip loss. For a large-diameter propeller, the idea is impractical due to the weight gained and the drag of the shroud itself which creates a net loss in performance despite the improved thrust. For the small ducted fan, fighting for whatever efficiency it

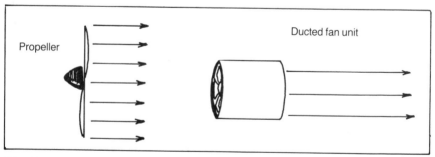

The characteristics of propeller thrust, left, and ducted fan impeller thrust, right, are very different. With the same size engine, the propeller accelerates a larger amount of air at a slower speed, while a fan accelerates a smaller amount of air at a higher speed.

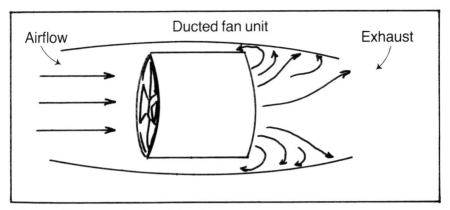

Ducted fan unit

Airflow

Exhaust

*Without the thrust tube, the airflow is
not directed and some exhaust air may
wander back through the fan.*

can get, the shroud would be inside the plane and weigh less. This is a positive gain. If a duct leading to the front of the fan and then to the tailpipe of the plane is also installed, drag loss in the thrust flow from fuselage interference and nondirected flow inside would be subtracted. Another plus for efficiency.

The shroud also serves several other purposes. First and most important, the shroud aims the airflow over the blades more efficiently. Each of

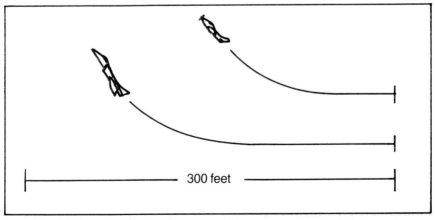

300 feet

*Relative takeoff characteristics of prop
planes versus fan planes. Prop aircraft
experience quicker acceleration than*
*fan aircraft and can takeoff in a
shorter distance.*

This photo shows the basic configuration of an engine mount. On this Dynamax unit, the slots are the housings for the stator blades which screw into it. The engine rests on the block section to the rear of the cylinder.

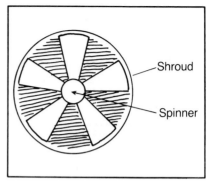

Fan swept area. The shaded area shows the swept area which does not include the hub spinner.

the blades on the impeller is really a small wing and like any other wing, it shares common problems. One problem is aspect ratio (the ratio of the wing's span to its mean chord or width):

$$\text{Aspect ratio} = \frac{\text{wing span}}{\text{mean chord}}$$

The problem with aspect ratio is that when it is low, say 2:1, the induced drag, or drag created by the thrust produced, goes up. The aspect ratio of

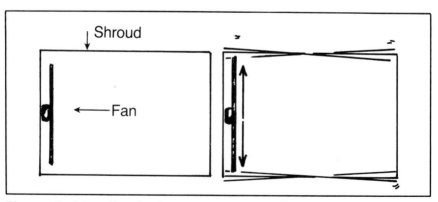

The practical impeller tip clearance shown on the left is between 1/32 inch and 1/6 inch. This clearance is necessary to allow for any blade wobble or stretch.

impellers is this low or lower. Consequently, the need for efficiency. With the shroud and a properly designed impeller, the ducted fan can work at a theoretical seventy to eighty percent efficiency in accelerating all the air it takes in.

The ideal separation between the impeller's blade tips and the shroud is zero. Yet at the high operating rpm, the impeller is subject to some vibration, wobble and blade stretch, and so blade clearance is necessary. The most practical separation between the shroud and the blade tips then is $1/32$ inch. Up to $1/16$ inch is acceptable but anything beyond that allows tip loss to build and negates the effect of the shroud.

Next on the list of shroud functions is that of mounting device. Most commercial ducted fans have an aluminum L bracket attached by screws to the shroud, allowing it to be mounted on horizontal rails in the same way that a glow engine is mounted to an airplane. Other fan units mount in a fitted circular cutout in the main fuselage former.

Because it also serves as the main support for the engine's weight and bears its dynamic loads, the shroud must be strong, rigid and light. Most early ducted-fan units used fiberglass-reinforced nylon as the basic material of the shroud and other components. With the advent of new composite materials, carbon fiber is now used to reinforce the nylon. It is lighter and stronger.

Inside the shroud, the impeller provides thrust through a combination of black magic and basic theory. There are numerous variables working to-

The Dynamax impeller on the left shows a greater solidity than the Vio-jett impeller on the right. Solidity can *be simply defined as the total swept area minus the total area of the fan blades, or as density of the impeller.*

27

gether or at odds with one another, requiring exacting and involved computations to create an impeller that is efficient and utilizes all the engine's horsepower. There are also some important structural considerations because of the high rpm used.

While early homemade impellers of plywood or stamped aluminum worked with the low power of early glow engines, today's powerhouses require greater precision. Several key words provide guidance to an impeller's function and its use of horsepower.

The first is fan swept area. A shroud may be five inches in diameter and the impeller slightly less, say 4.92 inches. The fan swept area is the area determined by the diameter of the fan minus the area taken up by the hub or spinner. This has a direct relation to determining the area of the tailpipe opening, the takeoff distance and the top end speed of the airplane.

Solidity is important because it determines the amount of horsepower a fan of given diameter can absorb. Solidity is the total fan area taken up by the combined total area of the fan blades. This has a bearing on the actual amount of thrust for a given size fan unit. The first Scozzi fan was approximately five inches in diameter and used five blades to absorb the 2.1 horsepower of the racing .40 engine. Some of the latest fans, such as the Dynamax and the Viojett, are almost the same size but use engines that put out four-plus horsepower. If not for the increased solidity of these impellers with their seven blades instead of five, the impeller would provide no thrust at all, overspeed and wreck the engine.

For those who use propellers regularly, pitch is a common term, defined as the theoretical distance advance of one revolution of a prop. For example, a propeller of six pitch might ideally advance six inches because of the thrust effect of one revolution of the prop. Because there are problems with drag and other inefficiencies, the real world effect is only about eighty-five percent of the theoretical pitch. Increasing the pitch allows greater final airspeed but inefficient thrust production at low speed. Decreasing pitch yields slower final speed but the propeller will be more effective at producing thrust at takeoff, climb or slow speed. Impeller design must then carefully balance the takeoff acceleration with the desired top end speed.

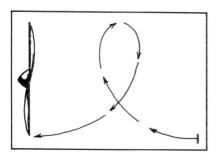

The theoretical distance traveled by a nominal eight-inch prop in one revolution is eight inches.

As an example, consider a full-size airplane with a variable pitch propeller allowing changes to the individual blade angles to use the propeller more efficiently. At takeoff, flat pitch is chosen so the engine can turn the propeller at full rpm permitting quicker acceleration (remember the car in first gear). If full pitch were chosen instead, the engine would not turn at full rpm, the prop would not function efficiently and the plane would accelerate slowly (remember the car trying to start in third gear).

The final design consideration is the desired rpm of the impeller. Since the impeller is a propeller with many blades, it works with the same basic thrust equation that a prop does:

$$\text{Thrust (T)} = \rho \, (\text{rho}) \times D^4 \times \text{rpm}^2$$

D = diameter of the prop
ρ (rho) = the density of the air
rpm = revolutions per minute

As you can see, the diameter of the propeller has a large influence on thrust. If we figured the thrust of an eleven-inch propeller and a five-inch propeller both turning at the same rpm, it would be obvious that the bigger prop provides much more thrust. Even if we doubled the rpm of the five-inch prop and held the rpm of the eleven-inch prop at the original speed, the larger prop would still create more thrust.

This bit of elementary aerodynamic mathematics shows why such high rpm are needed in a fan system. To recover some of the thrust capability of

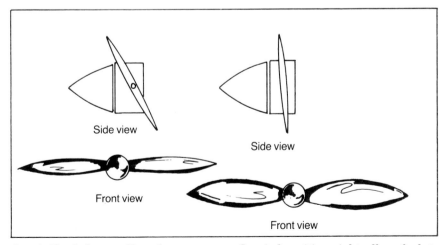

A variable pitch prop allows for a gross pitch position, left, which is better for cruising thrust yet poor for takeoff. The flat pitch position, right, allows for better static thrust, good for takeoff and poor for cruising.

the large propeller, the multibladed prop of a fan system must spin at high rpm—anywhere from 18,000 to 24,000—to achieve adequate thrust levels. Yet the prop must also travel at an efficient speed.

Compare the tip speed of an eleven-inch propeller turned at 12,500 rpm and a five-inch fan impeller turning at 22,000 rpm by using the following equation:

$$\text{Tip speed} = \frac{\text{circumference} \times \text{rpm} \times 60}{63{,}360}$$

circumference (in inches) = $2\pi r$
63,360 = conversion factor to miles per hour

The eleven-inch propeller tip turns at a little over 400 mph. To reach the same tip speed, a five-inch fan would have to turn at 29,000 to 30,000 rpm, a figure well beyond any glow engine's capability. The higher mph figure produces more thrust because like any wing or airfoil, more velocity provides more lift, especially if the airfoil shape has been matched to the best lift-to-drag ratio at that speed. Consequently, most impellers are designed for tip speeds in the 300 to 325 mph range which matches the horsepower peak of the glow engine.

Now that the fan impeller has accelerated the air, something must straighten the swirling flow, otherwise the disturbance from this swirl would rob thrust efficiency in the form of drag. This is where stators come in. Stators are situated behind the impeller, carefully angled and twisted so that the airflow meets the leading edge of the stator with the minimum amount of disturbance and is gradually turned from a swirl to a straight rearward flow.

Stators provide support for the fan shroud and in most of today's ducted fans, stators also provide the necessary mounting for the glow engine behind the impeller. Almost all fans have a single set of stators, although one system uses two sets of stators, one in front of the engine and one behind it. This dual-stator arrangement provides a steady, rigid mounting. The stators in front of the engine take out most of the swirl while the stators behind the engine take out some of the disturbed flow from the air passing around the cylinder of the engine.

Each fan unit has a different number of stator blades, which doesn't correlate to the number of blades on the impeller. The number of stators is dependent instead on the support required for the engine mount and efficient swirl recovery of the airflow. Like impeller blades, the pitch, chord and total area are a result of involved calculation. The basic requirements include the proper angle position to meet the incoming airflow, the proper distance behind the impeller (too far away and the flow becomes too disturbed for the stators to straighten the flow without a loss of energy) and the correct amount of area (too much and the drag cuts thrust).

The engine mount and fairing is a subtle but important part of the entire unit which is often overlooked. The fairing provides the actual mount for the engine and ties into the stators in the fashion engineered for the individual unit. Rigidity is a must. Most fairings are made of glass-filled nylon like common engine mounts. One other model is a massive cast aluminum piece. The mount also serves as a fairing to smooth airflow past the underside of the engine.

In the attempt to continue improving the fan's efficiency, the Viojett is the first unit to utilize fairings over the cylinder head, the aft engine area and the tuned pipe to minimize turbulence losses caused by these obstructions. It's been estimated that all these disruptions can cut ten to twenty percent of the thrust.

These thrust losses bring up the controversial subject of engine placement: before the fan (pusher fan) or behind the fan (tractor fan). Of the five American-made ducted fans, only one places the engine before the impeller. Of the three European fans, two place the engine before the impeller. The logic for engine placement before the impeller states that it is easier to set up and that a clear, unobstructed thrust flow is most important.

The majority of American manufacturers favor engine placement behind the impeller, reasoning that a clear, unobstructed airflow to the front of the fan is more important. They also argue that the thrust airflow provides better powerplant cooling, is easier to clean up with aerodynamic fairings, provides better placement of the fan unit with respect to the center of

Pusher and tractor fans are exhibited by the pusher Byro-Jet fan on the left and the tractor Axiflo 20 fan on the right. Both are presented in front views.

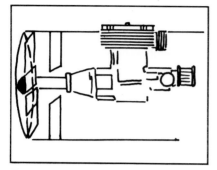
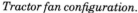

Tractor fan configuration.

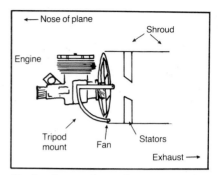

Pusher fan configuration.

gravity of the airplane and, most importantly, allows for an unobstructed intake.

For those making a choice, the options are still determined by the thrust characteristics of each unit and the requirements of the airframe.

Inlet, intake and exhaust

The ductwork to the shroud, impeller and exhaust is as important as the ducted fan itself. Its significance is in shaping and defining the column of air which the fan unit will work with. The ductwork adds to the complexity of the model, making it a structure within a structure, almost like building a boat in a bottle.

Most of the ducted-fan designs of today get by with a simple exhaust tube called a thrust tube. The more complex intake is generally avoided and compensated for by the cheater hole. The complexity of each design is governed by the efficiency required or desired.

The thrust tube is essential. Without it, we are back to putting a propeller on the front of our model jets. Once the airflow leaves the shroud as

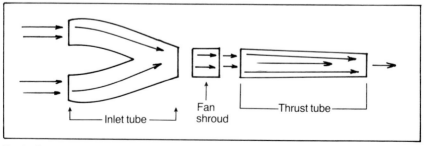

Basic duct components.

thrust, it must be directed and contained. Without the thrust tube, the flow can wander through the rear fuselage losing up to fifty percent of its energy in turbulence and the increased area of the rear fuselage. The design of the thrust tube must be efficient and certain parameters are essential. The most obvious one is the tailpipe opening which relates to the fan swept area. It also determines how fast the plane can go. Practice has found that the tailpipe should not be contracted or closed beyond ninety percent of the fan swept area. Constricting the tailpipe further chokes the exhaust flow and limits thrust because of the turbulence created. There's a popular analogy used to illustrate the example. Everyone is familiar with garden hoses. If you close the nozzle, the stream of water shoots out faster. If you leave the nozzle open, the water stream is slower. The same volume or amount of water flows, but the rate changes.

Keeping the tailpipe area between 100 and ninety percent of the fan swept area provides the model with its best static thrust, the type of thrust

Proper tailpipe diameters are essential to thrust. A good thrust tube, as pictured on top, includes a tailpipe diameter of about 90 percent of the fan swept area. A poor trust tube has too narrow of a tailpipe, choking the flow and stalling the fan.

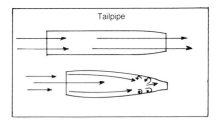

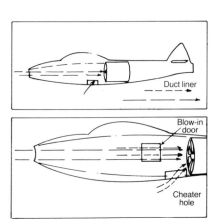

A cheater hole can be important; if the inlet is too small, it allows insufficient airflow for the fan's demands. To compensate, a cheater hole or blow-in door is added to satisfy the airflow requirements.

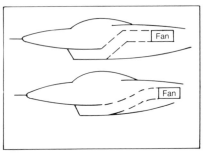

Inlet angles must also be carefully crafted. A poor inlet, top, may have too sharp an angle causing disturbed flow. A good inlet, bottom, will have smooth directional transitions and constant volume to create non-turbulent airflow.

which gives the best takeoff acceleration. It lets the fan move the air with the least amount of resistance. Modelers who want more speed from the same type of fan unit experiment with necking down the tailpipe up to as much as seventy percent of the fan swept area. This figure is regarded as the limit before the flow of the airstream chokes and efficiency rapidly dwindles.

Entry of the air into the ducted fan system is also important. In full-size jets with internal engines, the inlets and intake ducts are an elaborate design with careful contours and special ramps designed to lead the air to the engine with minimum disturbance. These full-size inlets must function in a wide range of flight conditions, from slow to supersonic speeds.

Models don't have to deal with such problems because the top speed ducted-fan models reach is only 150 mph, well below the speeds that absolutely require complex inlet-intake structures. Because of the speed and the extra complexity of an inlet-intake duct structure, many of the early scratchbuilt and commercial kits relied on the scale opening plus a cheater hole to provide sufficient flow to the fan. Without a cheater hole, only a certain amount of air at a certain speed can enter the fuselage. Once inside, the flow slows down because of the increased volume of the fuselage. The fan impeller works inefficiently because it cannot get enough air for thrust to reach the speed it is trying to generate. To compensate for the choking and to avoid using grossly oversize inlets which would ruin the scale appearance, modelers cut openings in the fuselage or nacelle in which the fan was housed to allow the fan to breathe. For appearance's sake, these cheater holes were cut in the bottom of the fuselage or nacelle just forward of the fan shroud.

The rectangular cutouts on the bottom ducts of this F-15 serve as cheater holes to supply sufficient airflow to the fan.

On this Byron Originals BD-5, the outlines on the side of the fuselage and the top of the canopy are blow-in doors. These spring-loaded doors remain closed when the engine is at idle or stopped. As power is applied, they gradually open inward to supply adequate airflow to the fan.

An alternate method to avoid sucking in runway debris, pebbles, grass and so on, is the so-called blow-in door. This is a panel cut out of the fuselage, usually on either side forward of the fan, and which is then reattached with a spring. At idle, the doors remain closed, but as demand for air is increased with advance of the throttle, the doors open inward to allow air to enter the fuselage. More complex than a cheater hole, the blow-in door is easier than engineering and installing an inlet-intake.

The ideal situation is a full inlet-intake tube system to provide the fan maximum thrust with minimum loss. Only recently have such systems appeared, thus eliminating the need for cheater holes or blow-in doors. The shape of the inlet lip is important, primarily at takeoff and low speeds. When the throttle is advanced to full takeoff power, a low-pressure region is created in the area in front of the inlet as the fan accelerates the air. Air is drawn from the front, top, bottom and back of the inlet to satisfy the demand for air. Without properly contoured curves to the inlet, the airflow above, below and in back of the inlet cannot negotiate the change in direction into the intake duct. If the inlet lip is too sharp, the flow cannot make the turn, creates turbulence and inhibits the airflow.

The inlet lip shapes now used are similar to the leading edge of a wing and, just as on a wing, if the leading edge is too sharp or too thin, changes in the direction of flight will disrupt the smooth flow of air. As the model accelerates, the flow of air into the inlet gradually changes to a straight flow. But the shape is still important as it allows the plane to maneuver and keep the flow aimed into the duct.

Once in the duct, the air has to be led to the front of the fan. It doesn't matter if the inlet shape is square, round or triangular as long as the change to the circular shape of the shroud is done without abrupt changes and the cross-section area of the duct is always the same. A general rule of thumb is

This profile shot shows the carefully molded curvature of a Violett inlet lip. Just like the leading edge of a wing, *this inlet lip is responsible for starting the smooth flow of air from all directions into the inlet.*

This is the Turbax I fan unit. It uses a .40–.46 engine and is classified as a five-inch fan. It turns in the 20,000 rpm range. With a revised engine mount, it becomes the Turbax III which uses a .65 ci engine to turn the impeller at 23,0000 rpm.

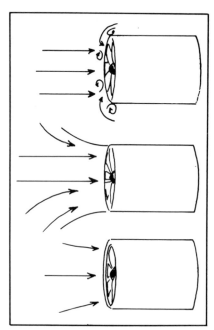

Inlet edges are critical for static thrust. A fan with a sharp-edged shroud, top, will create a turbulent airflow as the flow direction changes abruptly when entering the shroud. The effect is a deadening of thrust. A bellmouth opening, middle, allows a smooth airflow and no turbulence because the directional changes are smooth. The effect is good thrust. A shroud with a rounded mouth, bottom, creates no turbulence either, although the effect is not as pronounced as with the bellmouth. The inlet problem is alleviated once the plane accelerates.

This photograph shows how the stators tie into the engine mount. Mount is from a Turbax I, and is cast and machined aluminum. Stators are cast glass-reinforced nylon. Long screws run through a hole in the shroud down the length of the stator and are fastened by a nut inside the mount.

not to exceed a ten-degree offset angle from the inlet to the front of the shroud. This ensures that any curves necessary in the intake duct will not be too abrupt.

As far as the inlet area is concerned, the requirements are a compromise of scale appearance (when it applies), inlet shape and intake duct design. Areas run from as much as 200 percent of the shroud diameter down to ninety percent, or the fan swept area. In some commercial kits, these areas are predetermined by calculation and proven by operation. For those designing their own aircraft, trial and error or imitation of current intake designs are the only alternative for eliminating the need for a cheater hole.

Commercial fan units

Turbax
The Turbax I fan unit is a five-inch, aft-engine unit which was the original Scozzi fan introduced in the early 1970s. Since Jet Hangar Hobbies began marketing the fan, a second version, the Turbax III, was introduced in the early 1980s. Both units use the same five-blade impeller with the same

The O.S. 46 has become popular for the Turbax I because of its rear carburetor. It does, however, require the prop shaft *extensions shown in the left of the photo.*

shroud dimensions, the difference between the two being the engine mounts. The Turbax I was designed to use the .40 to .46 ci engines, and features an aluminum engine mount. The Turbax III was designed to use a larger .65 engine for additional rpm and thrust, so the engine mount was modified.

The shroud, impeller, impeller spinner and six stator blades are all made of glass-reinforced, injection-molded glass nylon. Two aluminum L brackets on the centerline of the shroud mount the unit on rails parallel to the shroud. The aluminum engine mount for the Turbax I is predrilled for the K&B 7.5 #9100 fan engine. To use the O.S. Max .46 VF-DF engine, a slight modification is required and an additional 1/4-28 by 1 1/2 inch socket or hex-head bolt must be purchased. The engine must also be aligned, the mounting holes drilled and tapped.

As with all fan units, assembly is required but it is relatively simple. The most difficult part is the engine mounting for the O.S. Max engine and drilling the holes in the L brackets for mounting. It's one of the most inexpensive fan units and because it was the first, many kits have been designed around it.

Byro-Jet

Introduced in 1978, the Byro-Jet fan was designed to power a line of large, scale jet kits manufactured by Byron Originals. It was also the second

Classified as a six-inch fan, the Byro-Jet is a pusher fan with a unique engine tripod mount. The fan spins 19,500 rpm with the Rossi .81 or 0.S. .77VR DF, and can produce up to 12 pounds of thrust. It has found favor with larger, single-engine ducted fan models and some very large scale twins. The shroud has a bellmouth shape on its front lip to help airflow into the fan because of the disturbances of the engine in front of the fan.

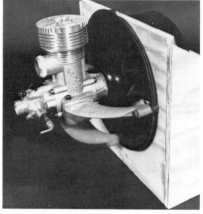

Shown in a test cradle, the Byro-Jet relies on bulkhead mounting. The screws which fasten the tripod to the shrouds also fasten the entire unit to the fan bulkhead.

commercial unit to become available, and provided a thrust unit for larger planes. The six-inch (nominal) fan originally used .60 to .65 ci engines to turn at an rpm of 16,000 to 17,000, providing about eight to nine pounds of thrust. In 1982 the Rossi .81 fan engine became available and significantly boosted the thrust output to eleven to twelve pounds at 19,000 rpm. In late 1986 the Rossi was discontinued and since then the new O.S. Max .77 VR-DF with the Byron cooling head has taken its place.

Like the Turbax fans, the Byro-Jet impeller, stators and shroud are glass-reinforced nylon, as is the engine mount. Unlike the Turbax unit, the Byro-Jet is a pusher fan. The engine is mounted in front of the impeller on a tripod that attaches to the front of the shroud. This tripod comes predrilled for a number of engines and can be ordered for any one of them.

Unlike any other fan unit, the Byron shroud is unique because of its bellmouth shape. The front lip of the shroud is curved to help airflow at takeoff and low speeds. This bellmouth shape is similar to that used in the static test stands of full-size gas turbine jets. This fan finds its primary use where good static thrust is needed, but it does rely on a cheater hole since any inlet or ducting advantage would be lost with the obstruction of the forward-mounted engine and tuned pipe.

Assembly is simple since the shroud and stators are a single injection-molded piece, as is the five-bladed impeller. The most difficult part of the assembly is aligning and attaching the entry cone to the front crankcase of the engine. This ABS plastic piece takes the place of the spinner in rear-mounted fans and covers the hub of the impeller.

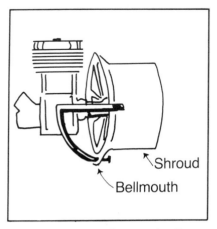

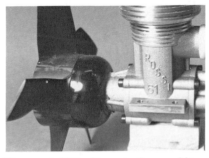

The bellmouth inlet on the Byron pusher fan is needed to compensate for the turbulent airflow due to the front-mounted engine.

The most difficult part of assembling the Byro-Jet was shimming and fastening the ABS plastic entry cone onto the front housing of the engine. It's fastened with a silicone sealer.

Instead of mounting on rails, the Byro-Jet requires a bulkhead with a circular cutout the diameter of the shroud. The shroud is inserted in the cutout and attached to the bulkhead with the same three mounting points as the engine tripod.

Because the line of eight Byron Originals jets uses this unit exclusively, it has become quite popular. It also has been used in the larger scratchbuilt single-engine models because of its good static thrust capability and its larger diameter which allows it to move a greater mass of air.

Axiflo, RK series

Shortly after the Byro-Jet was introduced, Bob Kress of Kress Jets introduced a line of Axiflo ducted fans designed for a variety of aircraft sizes and applications. It included the .051-powered RK-049, the .21 RK-20, and the .45 RK-40. Like the earlier Scozzi Turbax and Byro-Jet, each of the three Axiflos used a five-blade impeller and followed the popular route of the aft-mounted engine.

Only the RK-20 still survives. The RK-049 required extensive construction and had an application in only one small airframe. It produced thirty ounces of thrust but limited itself to a minimal airframe. The RK-40 experienced production problems and competed with the more popular Turbax I. The RK-20, with a four-inch fan, found use in a number of single-engine designs which are still available and in some twin-engined scale jets.

The RK-20 requires more assembly than the other fans since it uses two sets of stators, one in front and one behind the engine. The engine is completely enclosed by the long shroud, and the plastic parts are nylon. One of the unique aspects of the RK-20 is its integral fuel tank which is a streamlined bulb that mounts in the hub of the aft set of stator blades. It solves a problem of fuel placement so that the fuel draw is reliable. Much more so than conventional propeller planes, ducted fans wind up with fuel tanks in inconvenient places.

With the K&B 3.5 or the O.S. Max .25 VF-DF, the RK-20 can put out three-plus pounds of thrust. Kress, realizing that the four-inch fans had a good size application for smaller twins, was the first to start the trend toward stuffing more horsepower into the same size fan. In 1983, he introduced the RK-740, a four-inch fan that was even slightly smaller than the RK-20 in diameter but which had seven blades on the impeller instead of the common five. With the increased impeller solidity, the new 740 could effectively use the horsepower of the .45 engines like the K&B 7.5 and the O.S. .46 VF-DF and claimed a five-pound thrust output.

The 740 shares some of the same design features as the RK-20 such as two sets of stators, an integral center-mounted fuel tank and a long shroud which encloses the engine. The 740 introduced what has become a design feature of the latest high-performance fans, a multipart impeller with locking rings fore and aft which capture each of the seven individual blades. This feature has become a practice because the mold costs become prohibitively expensive for anything over five blades. It is less costly to design a single precision-molded blade and then engineer a hub mechanism to hold the blades in place.

Since its original introduction, the RK-740 has undergone several revisions. It is the most difficult of the fan units to assemble and the original version used a tin sheet-metal shroud which had to be rolled and bolted in place. Since then the sheet-metal shroud has been replaced with a one-piece fiberglass shroud which keeps blade tip clearance equal. This shroud can be retrofitted to the original RK-740 series.

For top performance, both the RK-20 and the RK-740 must have some sort of inlet. Without it, the performance of the fans suffers, primarily be-

Molded of nylon, the Axiflo 20 fan unit is the smallest of the current ducted fans. Using .21–.25 ci engines, the fan turns 21,000 rpm and puts out 3.5 pounds of thrust.

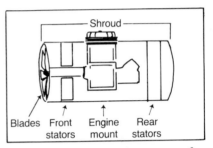

The RK-20 boasts a unique tractor fan arrangement with an elongated shroud to control both the airflow and subsequent thrust.

The RK-740 impeller requires extensive assembly and must be carefully balanced. The blade roots feature overlapping leaves held together with screws and a front and rear aluminum ring on the hub.

To help smooth airflow, the Axiflo series and the RK-740 can use foam accessory inlets as shown here. The Axiflo 20 also has a foam thrust tube, useful in podded engine applications.

41

cause the shroud lip is so thin and sharp and the impeller so close to the front of the shroud that without an inlet to guide the air to the fan, the flow becomes disruptive.

Dynamax

One year after Kress introduced the RK-740, Tom Cook of Jet Model Products introduced the Dynamax fan unit. Like the RK-740, the Dynamax unit took a fan size—in this case the five-inch fan—and designed it to absorb more horsepower. The Dynamax unit grew out of Cook's need for more thrust in the same size fan package for his large-scale F-4 Phantom kit.

To achieve that thrust, Cook chose to increase the solidity of the fan to absorb up to four-plus horsepower which could be provided by the Rossi .65, O.S. Max .77, or Rossi .81 RC RV. That accounts for the eleven impeller blades. These have a flatter pitch or twist than other high-performance fans but can yield ten pounds of static thrust. This fan unit has found a great acceptance as a good compromise between all-out performance and good takeoff acceleration.

Just as the RK-740, the Dynamax uses a locking hub mechanism because of the eleven blades of the fan. An aluminum hub and a forward ring capture the individual precision-molded blades. Because of the 22,000 rpm which the fan turns, the foot attachments of each blade are substantial. A complication to the design of any fan is ensuring that there is sufficient attachment area of the blade to the hub so there is no possibility of a blade

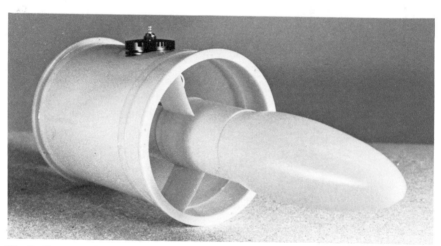

The bulb protruding from the rear of the Axiflo is the fuel tank. A secondary purpose for the bulb is as a fairing. Since it holds only six ounces, the tank is usually bypassed in favor of more remote fuel tanks which have more capacity.

Specifications

Fan Unit	Nominal Size (inches)	Hub Diam (inches)	Impeller Diam (inches)	Mounting Width (inches)	Greatest Shroud Diam (inches)	Length (inches)	Weight (ounces w engine)	Recommended Tailpipe Opening (inches)	Engine
Turbax I & III	5	2.169		5.3	5.26	5 5/32	26 (w engine)	4	.45 ci (I) .65 ci (III)
AXIFLO 20	4	1.770	4.19 (5 blades)	4.05	4.552	13 1/16 w fuel bulb		3 3/8	.21–.25 ci
RK-740	4	2.10	4.075 (7 blades)	4.235	6 7/8			3 3/8	.45 ci
Byro-Jet	6	2.295	5.945 (5 blades)	6 1/4	7 1/4	7 5/16	11	4 3/4	.65–.81 ci
Dynamax	5	2 5/16	5.0 (11 blades)	5 5/16	5 1/4	7	16	4	.65–.77 ci
Viojett	5	2.057	4.6 (7 blades)	5.135	5.745	6 3/8	14.5	3.4–3.6 (depending on inlet system)	KBV .72 or O.S. 77
Hurricane T6-25	6	2.25	5.875 (5 blades)	5 7/8	6.875 (topereal shroud)	6	16	4 5/8	Rossi .81 Picco 80 O.S. 79
T5-25	5	2.25	5.0 (5 blades)	5.0	6.250 (2 1/2° taper)	6	14	3 1/2–4	O.S. 46 ci K&B 7.5 ci
Boss 602	6	2.25	5.333	5.4	6.2	4.8	40 (w/Rossi 65)	4 3/4	Rossi .81 O.S. .77

shearing off. Since safety is paramount, some potential performance gains are sacrificed in the interest of safety.

To ensure the shroud stays perfectly round and also to provide a rigid engine support with a minimum of wobble, the Dynamax shroud has a single set of sixteen stators immediately behind the impeller. A precision-molded center section, called a turbine body, serves as the engine mount and ties the engine into the shroud with the impeller. Despite the high blade and stator count, the Dynamax is easy to assemble because all the reinforced nylon parts, such as the stator and impeller blades, are precision-molded to high tolerances. Perhaps the most difficult part of the assembly is ensuring the proper tip clearance of .02 to .03 in. With the fan in place, the tips are lapped to the shroud with sandpaper. Two aluminum L brackets on the side of the shroud are used to mount the unit to rails inside the fuselage.

Viojett

Perhaps the most sophisticated and advanced fan unit available is the nominal five-inch Viojett manufactured by Bob Violett Models. This unit has incorporated many refinements that have improved efficiency and reliability, and provided a level of high-speed performance that satisfies a fifteen-year-old promise made by Violett to engineer such a unit.

The first refinement has been in the materials category. The impeller blades, impeller spinner, stators and shroud are made of carbon-fiber-reinforced thermoplastic instead of the usual glass-reinforced material. The carbon fiber yields a stiffer and stronger blade, allowing the impeller to turn as high as 24,000 rpm without flexure or possible separation.

One of the more annoying characteristics of ducted fans is mixture adjustment of the high-speed needle valve because in most cases the shroud or the thrust tube encloses it. The Viojett incorporates a remote needle valve mounted on the outside of the shroud which makes adjustment easy and accurate.

The Boss 602 fan shows a high solidity and has excellent static thrust characteristics. A nominal six-inch fan, it has not become very popular in the United States although it's widely used in Europe. It takes a .65 to .81 ci engine, and its impeller is made of carbon fiber (earlier 601 fan was not made of carbon fiber).

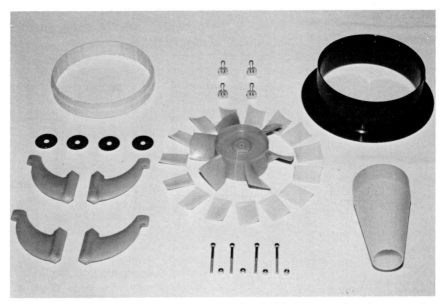

The Gleichauf fan is an imported German pusher unit in the nominal six-inch size. Shown with a dieselized Rossi .81, it uses a four-leg mounting system and a six-blade impeller.

To help dampen vibration, the unit uses rubber pads on the L mounting brackets. By absorbing some of the vibration, the chance for impeller wobble is minimized, which allows a smaller blade tip clearance for better efficiency.

The KBV .72 was jointly designed by Violett and K&B Manufacturing to provide the best horsepower conversion. To rigidly mount the engine in the shroud, Violett uses a massive single-piece cast-aluminum combination stator-cylinder head and fairing-engine mount. The aerodynamic fairing which encloses the cylinder head is actually a fat stator which serves a triple purpose.

First, it straightens flow like a stator. Second, it provides cylinder head cooling air through a milled slot. Third, its aerodynamic shape adds approximately ten percent more efficiency to the unit because it eliminates the drag and turbulence all aft-mounted engine fans experience from the aerodynamically unclean cylinder head. Because of its size, it also provides a rigid engine mount which helps lessen any chance of impeller wobble.

As part of eliminating the drag associated with airflow around the cylinder head, the shroud has been bulged just forward of the top of the cylinder so that there is no compression of the airflow. It helps maintain a constant cross-sectional area to the shroud similar to an efficient intake duct.

One other annoying problem with fan units has been tuned pipe adjustment. If the pipe overheats, the silicon couplers can soften and let the pipe adjustment slip, thus robbing the engine of peak horsepower and reliability. To solve this problem, the Viojett uses a tuned pipe with only two possible positions. One is for hot and humid or high altitude operation, while the second position is for normal weather operation. This pipe is also equipped with an aerodynamic fairing to shroud the pipe pressure line to the carburetor. As part of the overall efficiency, an aerodynamic center body fairing covers the aft-mounted carburetor.

Designed for maximum efficiency, the Violett inlet-intake system and thrust tube is a large part of the claimed eighty percent operating efficiency

Slightly smaller in diameter than the earlier Axiflo 20, the RK-740 is a four-inch fan that uses a .45 ci engine to produce five to six pounds of thrust at 21,000 rpm. Originally introduced with a sheet metal shroud, the MK III version now uses a molded-fiberglass shroud.

of the unit. To date, Violett has promoted use of the unit and been able to support performance claims only in his line of ultra-high-performance airframes since they are the only ones that can utilize the ducting. Still, the Viojett alone with all the fairings plus the KBV .72 (the O.S. Max .77 VR-DF is optional) is available separately for those who wish to use it in scratch-built designs.

Though the impeller for the Viojett consists of seven individual blades, it comes assembled and balanced. The KBV .72 also comes assembled and because many of the adjustment factors found in other fans like impeller balancing, needle valve adjustment and tuned pipe length have been engineered out of the assembly. Violett does not recommend running the unit on a bench stand as is done with others.

Miscellaneous fans and impellers

A review of fan systems available in the United States must mention some prototype and foreign units on the market. In some instances, they duplicate the thrust and sizes but offer alternatives to the scratchbuilder in terms of static thrust, mounting arrangements, or engine choice.

One caution is necessary. Any fan unit, including those already mentioned, should be evaluated on how widely it is used in designs. The old motto, "Let the buyer beware," applies. The products mentioned may be beyond some people's capability. Some of the fan units have not been suf-

The Dynamax fan unit is almost the same diameter as the Turbax I but can produce much more thrust. It's an example, like the RK-740, of stuffing more horsepower into a nominal diameter size. Using a .65 ci or .77 ci engine, it can produce up to ten pounds of thrust at 22,000 rpm.

The Dynamax impeller features the highest solidity of any of the American fans and has proven to be versatile in both high-speed performance and good static thrust capability.

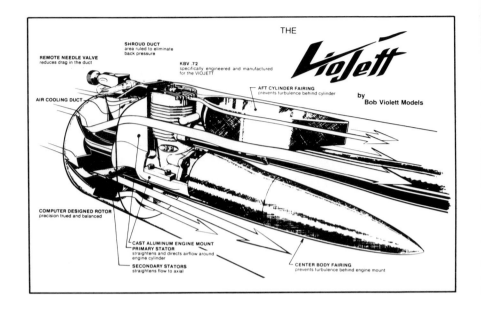

THE

VioJett

by
Bob Violett Models

SHROUD DUCT
area ruled to eliminate
back pressure

REMOTE NEEDLE VALVE
reduces drag in the duct

KBV .72
specifically engineered and manufactured
for the VIOJETT

AFT CYLINDER FAIRING
prevents turbulence behind cylinder

AIR COOLING DUCT

COMPUTER DESIGNED ROTOR
precision trued and balanced

CAST ALUMINUM ENGINE MOUNT
PRIMARY STATOR
straightens and directs airflow around
engine cylinder

SECONDARY STATORS
straightens flow to axial

CENTER BODY FAIRING
prevents turbulence behind engine mount

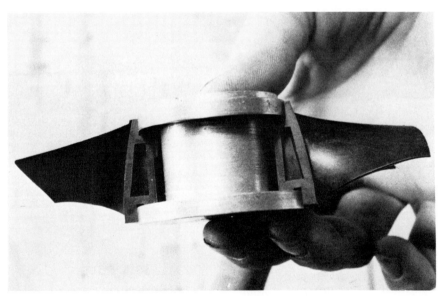

The later fan units have high blade counts on their impellers, and they usually feature an interlocking blade and hub design instead of a single-piece cast impeller. The Dynamx impeller shows the blade roots captured by the front and rear pieces of the aluminum hub.

ficiently proven and it's probably more prudent to wait and see before purchasing. Anyone involved with today's fans must understand that the high rpm and thrust levels demand some careful engineering using the proper materials. The days of the homebrew fan are over, except for those technically capable and sufficiently knowledgeable, because there's just too much danger involved.

Boss 602

This multibladed fan is an in-between size. With a diameter slightly over 5 1/4 in., it's in a category of its own, but it has been popular in Europe. The Boss has a high solidity with its twelve-bladed impeller and provides an excellent source of static thrust for high drag or large airframes because of the relatively flat pitch of the blades. Its top-end performance does not come close to American fans.

Designed in Sweden, it was originally the Boss 601 and was intended for .61 aft-mounted engines. When modelers tried to upgrade its power with the Rossi .81, it ran into blade shedding problems. While the impeller design could effectively use the extra horsepower, material strength and an extremely thin blade could not take the stresses incurred with the more powerful engine. The later Boss 602 incorporated a better blade locking design plus blades made from carbon fiber for the required stiffness. The Boss 602 is currently being marketed here in the United States by Kress Jets.

For the ultimate efficiency, the Viojett has incorporated refinements that other fans do not have. Designed primarily for use with its own KBV .72 fan engine, the unit puts out ten pounds of thrust at 23,000 rpm. It is a nominal five-inch fan and is designed for high performance. Bob Violett Models

Though it appears as a single cast piece, the Viojett is actually an interlocking blade and hub design which is factory assembled and balanced. The large hole in the spinner center is for the large hex-head spinner screw which is for starting the Viojett with the probe.

Rolf Gleichauf

Imported from Germany, this fan is a nominal six-inch-diameter unit and closely approximates the same mounting dimensions as the Byro-Jet. Like the Byro-Jet it is a pusher unit with the fan mounted in front of the impeller.

Its unique feature is a four-point mounting system to the bellmouth shroud. It has been recently introduced by JMI Imports, which is experimenting with the use of diesel model engines as powerplants. It also uses a

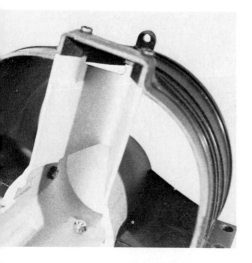

A massive single-piece aluminum motor mount fairing ties the engine into the shroud. It comes pre-assembled so engine alignment is already done for the modeler. Besides mounting the engine, the part also serves as an aerodynamic fairing. The slot at the top left side is for cooling air over the engine cylinder. Very effective.

One of the more desirable features of the Viojett is the remote needle valve mounted to the outside of the fan shroud. It saves the hassle of accu- rately locating a hole in the shroud for access to a needle valve or fiddling with a rear carb needle valve in the blast of the airstream.

six-bladed impeller with a single set of fifteen stators. So far, its only application has been with the Rolf Gleichauf F-16 kit also imported by JMI Imports.

Bauer

Another German import, this fan comes in two sizes. The Bauer 40/41 uses a .40 engine and is a nominal five-inch unit while the Bauer 60-91/81 uses a .60 to .90 engine in a nominal six-inch fan. Both are pushers but are unique in that there is some attempt to aerodynamically shroud the engine to improve airflow. All other pusher fans leave the engine and mounting legs exposed with no attempt to clean them up. The Bauer fans put a fairing around the lower rear crankcase of the engine and mount it inside the shroud on a substantial glass-reinforced mount.

The shroud is a durable glass-reinforced thermoplastic, as are the impellers, the fifteen stators and the stator ring. Another unique fact is the claim that the peak thrust output occurs at only 14,000 rpm for the smaller 40/41 and there is no need for a dedicated high-rpm fan engine. Because the Bauer fan has not been used extensively in the United States, it is impossible to verify the claim. The total weight of the unit is on the high side because of the large plastic pieces.

Hurricane

The latest ducted-fan unit is the American Hurricane fan produced by Steven Korney. Though still in the prototype stage, it offers a uniquely simple method of tailoring a fan unit and its impeller to either the peak horse-

Hurricane fan. This new concept features either pusher or tractor configurations for the three nominal size fans. The spinner-hub is machined aluminum, the blades are cast copolymer material and the shroud is a flexible nylon instead of the traditional rigid material. The unit can be bulkhead- or rail-mounted.

power of a specific engine or to the thrust requirements of an airframe. It comes as either an entire fan system complete with shroud, stators and engine mount, or simply as an impeller. There are three sizes, each in the standard nominal diameters of six, five and four inches.

The impeller can be tailored to a desired pitch or number of blades because of the two-part hub-spinner and the blade attachment design. The hub-spinner is aircraft-grade aluminum; precise slots are CNC-milled in the face of the hub to accept the impeller blade root which is then captured by the spinner screwed into the hub. Blade pitch can be altered by the angle that the slot is milled. The CNC equipment allows this. Because of the blade attachment method, there is also room to add more blades to increase solidity. One blade design can then be used to create completely different impellers, something impossible with the cast-glass nylon or carbon fiber impellers so widely used.

Hurricane impellers can be sized, by Korney, to fit some of the existing fan shrouds. His entire Hurricane fan units can also be configured in the tractor or pusher configuration.

If you are new to the fan market, the best advice is to stick to proven products which are in widespread use. There can be no quantum breakthrough because the laws of physics still apply and while there may be a faint glimmer that some ingenious modeler or designer may become the Einstein of ducted fans, it is highly unlikely. For now, nothing can substitute for rpm and a well-engineered strong fan unit.

Hurricane impeller. This picture shows the blade attachment method of the Hurricane fan with the aluminum spinner to the right. The impeller can be configured to ten blades and the slots are CNC-machined into the hub.

Chapter 3

Engines

Ducted-fan modelers owe thanks to the radio-controlled model boat fraternity for helping increase the thrust put out by modern fan units. It was the boaters' demand for high-revving engines in their racing boats which set the stage for current ducted-fan engines. The engine needs were similar: horsepower, strength, reliability.

These three conditions required major advances in model engine design, manufacture and materials before they could be realized. After the technology was proven in the boating field in the mid-seventies, it was incor-

This massive OPS .90 ci marine engine is characteristic of the marine engines from which fan engines are derived, as the basic layout is similar. Marine engines gave fan engines the rear carburetor, the rear exhaust and their relatively high-timed piston-liner combos.

porated in a modified form into the ducted-fan field. The Schneurle-ported engines with tuned pipes, rear carb and high exhaust timing became and remain the norm for fan as well as boat engines. The primary difference is in engine head cooling. Boaters rely on water-cooled heads. Fans use the traditional aviation air-cooled heads.

Like fan modelers, boaters use a small-diameter thrust device in the two-bladed boat prop. As in fans, the only way to overcome the thrust-limiting effect of the small prop is to significantly increase horsepower to reach the 24,000 to 25,000 rpm range (which could instantly pop to 30,000 rpm when the prop came out of the water) to bring properly designed boat hulls up to 60 mph speeds, and more.

Faced with diameter limitations—although not nearly as great—fan modelers took a look at boat engines with high rpm and realized that these engines were the answer to their own rpm desires. Of course, turning a four-to six-inch fan in the same 25,000 to 30,000 rpm range would exceed material strengths and impeller design because of the weight and size. A more conservative 20,000 to 24,000 rpm range was more desirable and with proper impeller design, could be attained.

Horsepower is the key to understanding how these engines work, and there have been many changes in engine technology to allow this. Horsepower is a misunderstood term, often confused with brute force. Horse-

A non-Schneurle O.S. .61 Blackhead, left, and a Schneurle O.S. .77VR-DF, right, shown together to illustrate the difference in case design of this type of porting. The pencil points to the extra bypass port cast in the crankcase by the Schneurle porting.

power can be understood as the rate at which a force does its work in moving something. For example, consider a person who must move a one-ton boulder a certain distance in a certain time, and a person who must move one ton of rocks the same distance in the same time. The first person must use brute force to move that single boulder. The second person does the same amount of work but the force required is less, yet the second person must work at a faster pace to accomplish the task.

This is true of the model engine as well. It achieves such high horsepower because it is doing a large amount of work at a fast rate. A lawn mower engine rated at the same horsepower as the model engine, on the other hand, has a job similar to moving the one-ton boulder. It does its work using a large amount of force at a slower rate. The basic equation for horsepower explains the relationship:

$$hp = \frac{T \times N}{5{,}255}$$

T = torque in pounds-feet
N = the shaft speed in rpm
5,255 is a factor

Torque is the force imparted to the engine crankshaft resulting from the pressure of the combustion process exerting leverage on the crankshaft pin. To maintain the same horsepower, or amount of work, torque must decrease and rpm increase, or vice versa, depending on the nature of the work to be done. To get more thrust, ducted-fan engines need the ability to reach high rpm, plus sufficient torque to keep loaded impellers spinning at these high shaft speeds.

Up until the mid-seventies, model engines could not provide what was needed for topnotch performance. Expert modelers would resort to hopping-up engines for maximum performance. Yet other factors such as reliability, broad operating ranges, long life and so on, diminished in direct relation to increases in horsepower.

Advances in technology revolutionized both model boat and model jet engines. Schneurle porting, ABC piston-liner construction, tuned pipes, PDP porting, investment cast molding, high-strength aluminums, synthetic oils, CNC machining, high-speed bearings, advanced intake and exhaust port designs all contributed to producing the high-horsepower, high-rpm engine. Better yet, these advances were incorporated in engines which were and still are reliable, easy to operate and, if properly maintained, live a reasonably long life. There were a number of advances in a number of directions that produced the desired result, backed by a push from an increasingly interested and growing number of modelers who wanted such engines for high-performance boats or aircraft.

If any single feature were identified as the main boost behind these powerhouses, it would be the Schneurle porting. Porting is the way the fuel-air mixture is introduced to the combustion chamber through passages in the crankcase and windows in the cylinder liner.

There were a number of methods used, the most common being cross-flow scavenging because it was easy and inexpensive to manufacture. It used a single fuel-air intake passage and port in the liner across from the exhaust port. Yet the scavenging was inefficient and could not fill the combustion chamber with the fuel-air mix needed for high power. The more fuel and air you can pack into the chamber and ignite, the more power you get.

Schneurle porting does it efficiently. It uses a main transfer port, directly across from the exhaust port, plus two boost ports set at ninety degrees on either side of the transfer port to pack in a dense, even fuel-air mix. Schneurle porting also loses less fresh fuel-air mix out the exhaust port than others. It was not incorporated because with the increased number of passages for the fuel-air mix, it was expensive and difficult to manufacture the required engine case.

One of the drawbacks, which Schneurle porting couldn't remedy for fuel-air introduction, was the area around the exhaust port which still suffered from a lean mix, robbing efficiency. Two technological advances

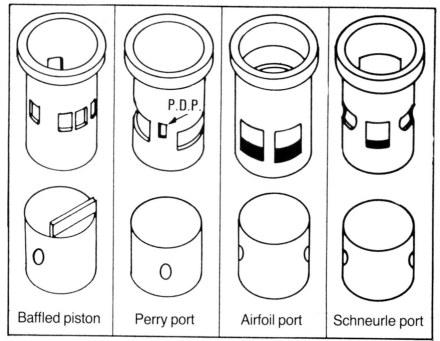

| Baffled piston | Perry port | Airfoil port | Schneurle port |

Porting arrangements.

56

helped here. The first was another method of porting called Perry Directional Porting which put small boost ports neighboring either side of the exhaust port itself and helped richen the mix in that region. The second advance was tuned pipes, a subject that will be explained later.

At first glance, a lot of this may seem common sense and unimpressive, but like the ducted fan and its associated duct system, we're dealing with highly directional flows which cannot afford efficiency-robbing turbulence. The area of the ports in the liner, their shape, their position and even the chamfer on their edge is important. Calculation and trial-and-error experimentation are all needed before the right proportions of areas, position and chamfer are found. Without them, a peaky engine results, or one that won't run at all.

To reach the rpm required for good thrust, a lot of the frictional losses in the engine had to be removed. Older engines of the seventies were ringed

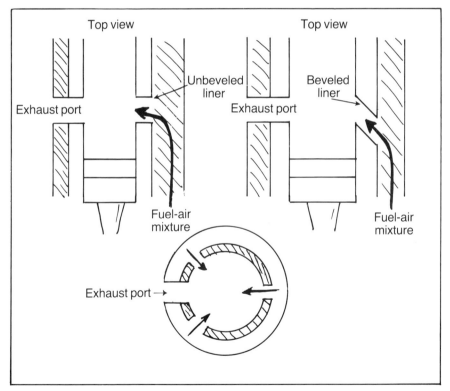

Beveled intake ports in the liner, right, provide a smoother fuel-air mixture flow to the cylinder head versus the un- *beveled intake, left, which allows the fuel-air mix to blow directly out the exhaust port.*

engines, easier to manufacture because of the materials involved. The compression seal relied on a ring in the piston which rode up and down the cylinder liner. It tended to generate friction which usually translates to heat and subsequent expansion. At the rpm range which these engines operated—usually 12,000 maximum—the friction and heat could be kept in control with lubrication and proper seating of the ring to the cylinder liner. If the heat got too high, the liner could distort, and compression could be lost. Loss of compression results in loss of power and loss of rpm. A more effective compression seal was needed before these high rpm could be reached.

The solution was the ABC piston-liner construction. It gives a piston-liner seal that adjusts for all heat conditions from low to high rpm. Its secret is in matching the thermodynamic expansion rates of three materials, aluminum (A), brass (B) and chrome (C). The liner is made of brass to which a thin surface coating of chrome is applied electrochemically. The piston is aluminum. The top of the cylinder liner is tapered so that the piston-liner fit is squeaky tight.

Turning over many ABC engines by hand is difficult since the fit is so tight at the top of the piston stroke. When the engine gets to operating tem-

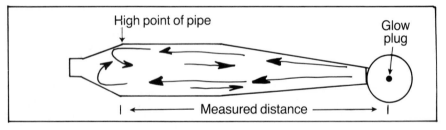

Tuned pipe theory states that the exhaust wave is reflected from the high point of the pipe to re-enter the glow plug and pack a fresh charge in the cylinder.

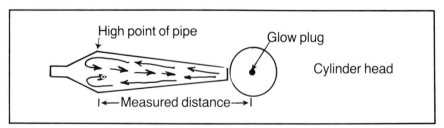

A peaky pipe allows the engine to only operate at a narrow rpm band due to incorrect timing of the reflected wave.

perature, the liner expands, but always at a rate slightly higher than that of the aluminum piston. Thus the seal always remains tight, even as the rpm and the operating temperature rise. Unlike the ringed engine, high heat conditions cannot damage the engine, since they are compensated for by the thermal expansion rates of the piston-liner materials.

Along with the Schneurle porting, the use of tuned pipes is the other major advance to contribute to the high rpm and enhanced efficiency of the new engine technology. Tuned pipes have added as much as 1,000 additional rpm to model engines, a significant gain. Far from being sophisticated mufflers, these devices have been compared to superchargers which are added to engine carburetors to pack as much fuel-air mix into the combustion chamber as possible.

Tuned pipes work on the wave propagated by the exhaust of a model engine to do two things. First, they help draw the fresh fuel-air mix into the combustion chamber before ignition, and then ensure a minimal loss of the

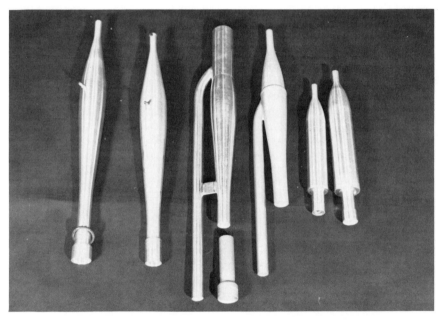

These are the tuned pipes generally used in today's fan engines. From left to right: the Dynamax pipe for Rossi .65 or O.S. .77VR-DF; the Viojett pipe for the KBV .72; the Byron pipe for the Byro-Jet plus the special telescoping header pipe for easy pipe adjustment; *the Rossi pipe for the Byro-Jet; the Macs Wizard pipe for the Axiflo 20 using either the K&B 3.5 or the O.S. .25 VF-DF; and the Macs Wizard pipe for the RK-740 or Turbax I using the K&B 7.5 or the O.S. .46VR-DF.*

fresh charge out the exhaust port. Besides being a significant power booster, it also can be a significant power destroyer if not understood.

Just like a pipe on an organ, a tuned pipe increases power by resonance of the exhaust wave. To achieve that resonance it must have the proper diameters, diverging and converging shape, and length to harmonize with the engine's rpm, displacement and peak operating temperature. There's not too much a modeler can do about the physical dimensions of a pipe. If properly selected to match the engine's characteristics, then all the modeler must do is tune the length of the pipe for the conditions the model will operate in.

If the tuning is off, destructive interference takes place and hinders power. First of all, as the exhaust gases exit the manifold into the pipe, a negative pressure wave is set up which actually sucks the gases out and draws the fresh fuel-air mix in. The wave continues to travel down the pipe, reaches the place where the pipe begins to converge, and some of the wave is reflected back to the exhaust port. If properly tuned, this positive pressure wave arrives in the nick of time to ram the fresh fuel-air mix back into the chamber without—hopefully—losing any of it. This ram effect conserves the density benefits gained by the Schneurle porting and magnifies the effect of the combustion process because there's more to burn.

One problem early users of pipes discovered was that the classical peak power pipe was extremely temperamental. It would only kick in its power boost in a narrow band of rpm because the wave was so precisely tuned. If throttling an engine were required, as in an airplane, the pipe would gurgle and struggle each time it came off its peak and it would be difficult to get it back on, blocking the engine's smooth operation.

The solution was the broad band pipe which diminished some of the boost effect but allowed engines to move from low to high throttle. By extending the portion of the pipe to a straight line where it begins to taper, it tamed the sensitivity of the pipe to rpm.

A tuned pipe can help any engine to a greater or lesser extent depending on the efficiency of design. But they do tend to favor and operate more reliably with engines that have an exhaust port duration timing of 155 to

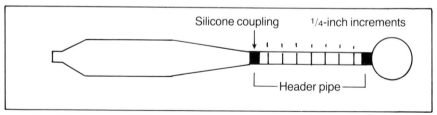

A pipe is properly tuned by cutting 1/4-inch increments from the header pipe until maximum rpm is achieved.

175 degrees. This simply means that for so many degrees of shaft revolution, the exhaust port remains open. Timing can go as high as 180 degrees and beyond, but this makes pipe operation sensitive again. Tied to the exhaust timing is the intake duration timing which runs 120 to 130 degrees.

These are considered high timings only because previous model engines used more conservative timings, probably because of porting inefficiency. For example, most non-Schneurle port engines, using cross-flow scavenging, had an exhaust duration timing of no more than 140 degrees and an intake timing of 100 to 110 degrees.

Tuning a pipe is a trial-and-error process, which has made engine-fan teststands popular. Several recent fan units have done away with this need, however, most notably the Viojett, with pipe-lengths matched to the engine and fan. A simple formula for getting a ballpark length figure is:

$$L_t = \frac{E \times V}{N}$$

L_t = the length of the pipe from the glow plug to the mean high point
E = the open exhaust period
V = the wave speed down the pipe (1,700 ft/sec)
N = engine rpm

You can see that for any given engine, as the rpm go up, the pipe length will get shorter. Pipes used with ducted fans definitely run shorter than a comparable piped-pattern engine.

Adjustment starts with the pipe and header at the longest length. The idea is to shorten the pipe distance until maximum rpm are reached. The pipe is not shortened; it is the header pipe bolted to the engine exhaust manifold which is gradually shortened by cutting no more than 1/4 inch increments at a time from the pipe. Once peak rpm are reached, the plane is flown to check the setting.

The tuned pipe is obvious. The glow plug is not. It's often overlooked as a beneficial item and can subtly but powerfully contribute to balky performance. The glow plug functions on the principle of catalytic reaction during the combustion process. Inside the plug body is the familiar coiled element. Depending on plug manufacture it varies in diameter from 0.006 to 0.008 inch, and can be straight platinum or a platinum-rhodium alloy. Once combustion is started by the glow plug with the assistance of the starter battery, it's maintained by the glowing element through the heat and catalytic reaction between the platinum and methanol in the glow fuel.

Since most high performance engines, especially ducted fans with high rpm, experience higher heat, chamber pressures and, most importantly, the higher frequency of combustion, these thin elements are subjected to a severe pounding. Consequently, glow plugs suitable for ducted fans tend to be on the cold side. That means they generally need a slightly higher voltage and current to start, and their catalytic reaction is subdued so that they

This picture shows the arrangement for retaining the header pipe. A steel ring fits over the flange of the header and a heavy-duty steel spring, attached to the ring, retains it.

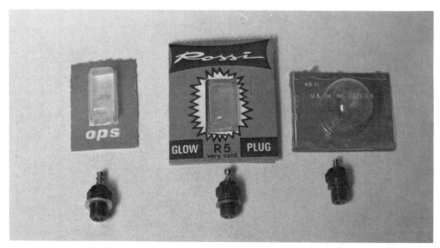

These are the most widely used plugs for the fan engines. They are designed to tolerate the heat, chamber pressures and rpm of a fan engine. They are generally known as "cold" plugs. From left to right: the OPS 300, the Rossi R-5 and the K&B-1L.

don't pre-ignite the fuel-air mix. They also need to have a stronger element to withstand the higher frequency combustion.

Compare this with the four-stroke model engine. Since the time between combustion strokes is almost four times as long in the slower-revving engine (usually turning at 10,000 rpm, of which only half are combustion strokes, while the fan engine can turn up to 25,000 rpm with combustion on every stroke) the glow plug must be hotter. It must retain heat from combustion and sustain the catalytic reaction for a longer time. If a ducted-fan engine used the same hot type of plug, it would risk detonation, prematurely igniting the fuel-air mix before it's ready for its pressure-exhaust stroke.

Consequently, choosing the right plug for the fan engine is critical. Several have proved themselves in a variety of engines, including the Rossi R5, the OPS 300, the K&B 1L, the O.S. #8 and the GloBee. For the higher-revving fan engines, 22,000 to 25,000 rpm, it has become a safe practice to change plugs every other flight, perhaps every flight, to ensure a reliable engine run. No matter what rpm, however, it is always safer to check the plug than to risk an engine flameout and a deadstick landing.

The internal duct and internal fan make fuel tank location and adequate capacity a problem. The larger engines gulp fuel at a rate of approximately 2 to 2.5 ounces or more. For a comfortable ten-minute flight with a margin of extra fuel in case of a go-around and to avoid sucking air, a twenty-four ounce fuel tank would be a logical choice. To date, ducted-fan modelers have made due with available tanks whose dimensions and shapes do not lend themselves to the space available.

Another problem is tank distance from the needle valve. The longer the distance, the poorer the draw. The centerline of the tank is also difficult to

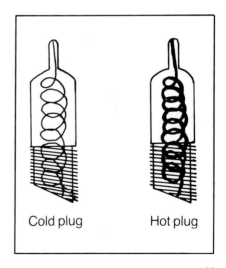

The performance of cold and hot glow plugs is vastly different. The cold plug element is designed to give less glow so as not to pre-ignite the fuel-air mixture at high rpm. The hot elements, meanwhile, glows more easily for good idle and low rpm running.

Cold plug   Hot plug

The saddle fuel tank system is becoming increasingly popular as a means of fitting fuel in the tight confines of a fan fuselage and keeping the fuel supply close to the engine. These Violett tanks have been specially molded to fit the confines of a fuselage and are reinforced with carbon fiber cord to prevent bursting, a possibility with a pressurized fuel tank.

Internal ducting often dictates a remote fuel tank position, so to keep fuel draw problems to a minimum and allow flexibility in positioning the fuel tank, some fan modelers rely on fuel pumps such as this Perry Canister pump, which works on crankcase pressure. It is designed to be remotely mounted.

maintain near the centerline of the needle valve as the tank must be kept out of the duct.

Despite these drawbacks several methods are employed. The tank employed in the Kress Jets series of ducted fans is a specially molded tank mounted as a center body fairing. Tank capacity is adequate for the smaller RK-20 but minimal for the RK-740 which uses a much larger .45 engine.

The Byro-Jet relies on a special adaptation of two commercial tanks which are usually suspended in front of the engine with the tank centerline at the same level as the needle valve.

Some installations rely on the use of a header tank. This is a small tank, usually only an ounce or two, which serves as the direct feed tank to the carburetor. It is fed by a larger remote tank. The advantage to this arrangement is that the small tank can be more easily positioned in an appropriate location and maintains a constant fuel level.

The latest method uses saddle tanks, which get their name from the way they straddle the duct like saddlebags on a horse. They were first employed in the Bob Violett series of sport-pattern planes, and feed the needle valve through common plumbing.

Attempts at using fuel pumps permitting a convenient, probably remote, fuel tank location have not fared well. The first use was the Perry pump and Perry carburetor on the K&B 7.5 ducted-fan engine. Because the pump actually replaced the rear crankcase cover, it was difficult to adjust to changing conditions since it was inaccessible when mounted in the plane, and operation was also erratic.

The Perry Canister pump is designed to run from crankcase pressure (not muffler pressure) and can be adjusted to flow requirements. It can be remotely mounted up to three or four inches from the needle valve. Its best application is for very remote tank locations.

Drilled into the side of the engine-mounting flange of this O.S. fan engine is a crankcase pressure tap. It supplies the required pressure to operate a pressure fuel pump.

Other pumps such as the Robart AutoMix Mark V, which works from crankcase pressure, have been tested but do not seem to provide sufficient fuel volume. The latest pump to be tried is the Perry Regulator, a canister-type pump which works from crankcase pressure, and can be mounted anywhere within three inches of the crankcase pressure tap. So far it's been used with varying success.

The early carburetors used with these engines presented some problems in terms of positioning on the engine, the ease of running a pushrod to the throttle arm and the amount of fuel they could deliver. Part of boosting power is the ability to provide a heavy charge of fuel-air mix. You could have the best cylinder liner-porting arrangement in the world but it would do you no good if you couldn't get the fuel there. To do that, the carburetor venturi must be enlarged so that more air and fuel can be drawn down the throat. This immediately diminishes suction and fuel draw through the needle valve because of the lowered pressure. It's not a bad problem if the engine is to be run wide open all the time like boat racers do. But if there is a need to throttle the engine as there is in aircraft, it means that opening and closing the throttle barrel is constantly changing the mixture.

It took time, but modern high-performance carburetors have sorted out the deficiencies of the earlier ones. Low-end and high-end needle valves help correct mixture. Precise carburetor barrel slotting aids mixture adjustment as the throttle is advanced from low to high speed. Helping the situation further is the fact that a low idle is not needed on a ducted fan. Even with an idle of 3000 to 4000 rpm, there is no significant thrust produced. On a propeller airplane, that kind of rpm would start a good taxi, even on grass.

Almost all the ducted-fan engines have gone to rear-mounted carburetors despite the increased parts count that results. In aft fan units, a rear carburetor is easier to access with cable-style pushrods and makes needle valve adjustment easier too, without having to get fingers close to an impeller turning at twenty-plus rpm. There's also a plus in the reduced drag an aft-mounted carb gives the fan unit. The carburetor body, needle valve and pushrod linkages are all out of the airflow. In the front-mounted fan unit like the Byro-Jet, a rear-mounted carb faces forward into the airflow. It too is easy to access for needle valve adjustment and direct throttle pushrod throw.

Unless you are looking for all-out performance (and expense in replacing engine parts) the fuel that's best for today's ducted-fan engines is a regular, high-quality sport fuel with no more than ten percent nitromethane. Modern high-performance engines have been designed with high compression ratios of 10:1 and up, and porting that favor a fuel without the bang which nitro gives. This design element is in keeping with the FAI regulations eliminating the nitro content of fuels used in international competition. Using a high nitro content of twenty percent or more will only risk detonation with attendant power loss, stress on engine parts and shorter engine life. For those who insist on maximum power and want to use a higher nitro content, most manufacturers either supply or have available an optional cylinder head shim which slightly increases the combustion chamber volume and lowers the compression ratio to cancel the possibility of detonation.

The only real requirement is to get a fuel which has a good, high-heat lubrication and additives to help prevent rusting. Synthetic fuels have largely replaced the role of castor oil as the prime engine lubricant but they still do not have the high-heat film strength qualities which castor oil has. Even at operating temperatures of 500 degrees Fahrenheit, castor will not break down as synthetics tend to do. The disadvantage of castor is its tendency to varnish and form carbon deposits. To get the best of both worlds, the high film strength of castor and the nonvarnishing tendencies of synthetic lubricants, the better ducted-fan fuels are a blend of both. The majority of the fuel's lubricant content is the synthetic, and usually about five percent or more castor oil is added to it.

Depending on manufacturer, other additives are incorporated in the fuel, often a rust preventative. It's of minor benefit, however, because of the methanol in the fuel which attracts moisture and acids formed by the burning of some of the synthetic lubricants. About the only sure rust-preventer is an after-run engine oil, whether it be a commercial product like Prather's or a simple light oil like Hoppe's gun oil. It's also necessary to empty the crankcase of as much residual fuel as possible by running the engine dry after you're finished flying.

Ducted-fan types

In the late seventies ducted fans and airframes came out of the experimental oddity stage to gain a foothold in the mainline world of modeling.

These are three of the four O.S. fan engines. From left to right: the O.S. .65VR-DF, the .46VR-DF and the .25VF-DF. With the exception of the small .25, all use rear carbs.

Many modelers, however, made the mistake of choosing economy when purchasing an engine. Unfortunately it was a false economy because they purchased inadequate powerplants and ended up losing their investment in a crash. Manufacturers were also to blame by claiming that their units could function with lesser and cheaper powerplants.

Remember that there can be no substitute for high rpm in a ducted fan, and immediate high rpm means a quality engine with more engineering sophistication than conservative sport engines. It does not mean frustrating experiences with sensitive, cranky engines. The engines cited below have proven themselves in operation. With intelligent use and maintenance, they will provide successful and reliable ducted fan operation.

O.S. Max VF-DF and VR-DF series

Of all engine manufacturers, O.S. Max has one of the most extensive lines of engines devoted to ducted fans. They do not have the reputation as all-out powerhouses but have always given reliable operation. As one modeler noted, the winner's circle is usually occupied by the one who stresses reliability and dependability.

O.S., in keeping with its philosophy of involvement in all facets of modeling, has provided a fan engine for every nominal size of fan unit.

For the small Axiflo RK-20, O.S. has provided the O.S. .25 VF-DF ABC. Based on the same crankcase as the .25 VF ABC rear-exhaust Schneurle engine, the .25 VF-DF ABC uses an ABC piston-liner with a higher exhaust port timing. The carburetor is a front rotor, mounted ahead of the engine

The latest O.S. fan engine, the .77VR-DR, can be used with the Byro-Jet, the Dynamax or the Viojett. Shown here with the large air-cooling head required for the Byro-Jet, it also comes with a standard air-cooled head for the other two fans.

cylinder on the front crankshaft housing. Despite the advantages of a rear-mounted carb, the application of this engine to the Kress Axiflo and the Aerojet .25 fan units does not allow the use of a rear-carb engine because of the center-mounted aft fuel tank position.

For the popular Turbax I and the RK-740, the O.S. Max .46 VR-DF has become increasingly popular. The carburetor is mounted to the rear crankcase cover with a rear-exhaust engine. This particular engine was adapted from the marine high-performance engines, the O.S. .40 to .46 VR-M ABC. When using the rear carb, O.S. has settled on a disk induction. This means that a disk driven by the crankshaft, with a precisely cut opening, allows the entrance of the atomized fuel-air mix into the crankcase.

For a long time, there were no rivals to the Rossi .81 engine as the engine of choice for the popular Byro-Jet unit until O.S. introduced the O.S. .77 VR-DF ABC engine in 1985. Since then it has overtaken the Rossi in the Byro-Jet application and become the favored engine in the Dynamax fan unit. Like its .46 forebear, it is a rear-carb, rear-exhaust engine and is equipped with the new O.S. 8B carburetor which has proven itself as a reliable throttle device with good response.

The .77 comes with choice of two cylinder heads. For the Byro-Jet application, it has a large heat sink head to provide sufficient cooling in the tur-

Using the same case as the Rossi .65, the Rossi .81 RV-DF became the standard engine for the Byro-Jet because it could turn the impeller to 18,000– 19,000 rpm for 12 pounds of thrust. It was also the first fan engine to offer a remote in-flight mixture adjustment.

bulent airflow of the forward-mounted engine of this fan. For the Dynamax, and if desired, the Viojett installation, the engine comes with a conventional cylinder head since the aft-mounted position of the engine in both units provides more than adequate cylinder head cooling.

Rossi

During the 1970s the imported Rossi engines were reserved for high-performance specialty modeling applications in plane and boat racing. As the raceboat hulls got larger, the engines had to increase horsepower correspondingly. Rossi kept introducing new engines, the most significant being the R61-65 in about 1979. Because it was proven on the racing circuit, the R65 marine version was adapted for the Byro-Jet unit because it could put out 3.5 hp at 24,000 rpm. Up to that time, the only other engines available were conventional, lower-powered pattern airplane engines.

The R61-65 is no longer used with the Byro-Jet but was the original engine chosen to power the Jet Model Products' Dynamax fan. It is primarily designed to run on FAI no nitro fuel, but if you prefer nitro, you can add a head shim and optional head insert. Without these optional parts, the engine can be damaged by detonation, or it will at least run raggedly.

Since the boating application of the engine favors a rear-mounted carburetor, it was easy to adapt to ducted-fan use with an air-cooled head. The carburetor was one of the first to employ a high-end needle valve which could be adjusted during operation by an independent servo. The need came from boaters using peaky pipes sensitive to minor changes in operating conditions. This feature adjusted the mixture while running so that a lean or rich run could be compensated for. Instead of the simple disk valve behind the carburetor as on the O.S. engines, the Rossi uses a rotary drum valve.

On first appearance the R61-65 case is massive. It was natural for Rossi to bore it out and put in a higher-displacement cylinder liner-piston-rod combination, and the R80 appeared in ringed and ABC versions. Byron Originals, looking for an even more powerful engine to give them better thrust-to-weight ratios, had Rossi manufacture a large air-cooled head which would work with the Byro-Jet. Since it was introduced in 1981, the Rossi R80 has been the preferred engine for the Byro-Jet. Early in 1986, however, production was discontinued. It can still be purchased but the supply is shrinking. Frequent maintenance parts like bearings, needle valves and gaskets are still available.

K&B

Credit must go to K&B Manufacturing for taking the early lead—and risk—of providing a dedicated ducted-fan engine. The K&B 7.5 #9100 with Perry pump and Perry carburetor was the engine that made the early Scozzi-Turbax fan-powered models practical. Introduced in 1978, it was an outgrowth of the K&B 40S racing engine first used with the Scozzi fan. The 40S had power, but it lacked several desirable features. It had only an exhaust throttle and had to be run at peak. At the start, K&B introduced the slightly smaller displacement K&B 6.5, but then went to the larger 7.5 to give what is now known as the Turbax I a practical 20,000 rpm. It defined what a basic fan engine should incorporate: rear exhaust; high-performance carb; strong, rigid but lightweight case; high-quality bearings; Schneurle porting; and ABC cylinder liner and piston.

At first the integral pump with the Perry carb was thought to be essential but adjustment proved difficult and the new versions deleted it. A new 9101 performance package was added with an advanced ABC liner and piston combination, a replacement backplate and a new carburetor to eliminate the Perry pump and carburetor combination. One of the drawbacks to the engine, despite the highest power rating for its class, has been the front rotor carb.

Shortly after the introduction of the 7.5, K&B introduced the 3.5 engine in a variety of configurations for cars, boats and aircraft. It followed the same layout as the larger 7.5 except that the Perry pump-carburetor combination was never installed. It probably still is one of the most powerful en-

K&B 7.5 cc #9100 fan engine.

gines in its class, and finds its only fan application in the old Axiflo RK-20 series designed by Bob Kress.

The most recent fan engine to be introduced is the KBV .72, a joint venture between Bob Violett Models and K&B Manufacturing. It uses much of the structure of the K&B 11 cc marine racing engine, but the displacement was purposely matched to the power requirements of the Viojett fan unit. A rear carburetor with rotor valve induction was installed instead of the 11 cc engine's front rotor carb. This carb uses the same body as the K&B 11 cc but Violett has modified the barrel to get around several problems experienced with fan carburetors.

The barrel is a one-piece machined shaft with the actual throttle arm screwed into a tapped hole at the end. There is no throttle setscrew (a small adjusting screw that stops barrel rotation) to eliminate a jammed barrel. Instead, the barrel is free to rotate 360 degrees. Some fan engine carburetors have had the tip of these throttle setscrews break and jam the barrel in all positions. But here, barrel rotation is determined by servo throw. A special slot has been milled into the surface of the barrel to help mixture adjustment during throttle transition, a problem with some fan engine carburetors.

The head of the engine is a special design used by Violett. Several other modifications have been incorporated to improve performance and adaptability of the engine exclusively to the Viojett.

In the background is the original #9100 K&B 7.5 cc engine with the pump and old Perry carb. In front of it *is the new piston, liner, carburetor and crankcase cover.*

OPS

There are a number of other engines which have been manufactured in displacements and power ratings to suit their application with today's popular fan units. The .80 displacement category has seen the most variety, the OPS .80 engine in particular. Known for marine racing engines and pattern aircraft engines, OPS adapted its .80 water-cooled marine engine with an air-cooled head. To date, the engine has not found widespread acceptance because of its high price. Although it is a powerful, strong, reliable engine, the front carburetor layout and the lack of a large air-cooled head have limited its application in the Byro-Jet and Dynamax fan units.

Picco

Picco has advertised three ducted-fan motors at attractive prices. They match the .80, .45, and .21 ci displacements and are considered powerful motors. They have yet to find widespread use in fan units.

Other power directions

The use of glow engines as the sole power source for a ducted fan has some difficult problems that are almost insurmountable: noise, high fuel

Based on the K&B 11 cc marine engine, the KBV .72 engine was designed exclusively for Bob Violett's specs for use with the Viojett. It incorporates a number of modifications, chiefly the addition of a new carburetor.

One of the main problems facing fan engine operation is the carburetor. The KBV .72 carb has a massive throttle arm to overcome the metal fatigue experienced by standard arms because of high vibration levels. It also has a specially milled barrel for smooth throttle transition.

The Picco 80. This engine has been modified and upgraded recently, and it now has improved internal porting, a new carburetor, new bearings in phenolic races and a bolt-on front crankcase. The horsepower rating is a whopping 5 hp.

consumption and duct drag. The noise problem has limited them to less noise sensitive fields. The high fuel consumption has complicated internal arrangement because of the tank dimensions required. Duct drag, because of the cylinder head, carburetor, pushrods and plumbing, robs a significant amount of efficiency.

As alternatives and solutions to these problems some modelers have been experimenting with other power sources. The most logical one to date has been diesel power. Proponents of this form of power point to the ability of diesel to provide the same power at the necessary rpm as the glow engine, while cutting down on noise. They also point to the well-known economy of diesel engines and their reliability because they eliminate the one source of potential trouble, the glow plug. Experiments with diesels and fans, however, is still too new to provide proven figures. One of the chief questions is whether engine components designed for the pressures and rpm of glow fuel

More of a curiosity than practical, the Kavan gas turbine shows some of the complexity required to power a model with a true gas turbine. The Jackman turbine, though simpler, is still highly complex to operate and would appeal only to a very limited group of modelers with technical backgrounds.

Not widely used, the OPS 80 is still a good engine. It has not been used primarily because of expense. The OPS has not been used in the Byro-Jet either because it does not have the necessary large air-cooling head.

operation can be modified to the higher internal pressures of the diesel at the same high rpm.

As nickel-cadmium battery technology continues to improve and cell size and weights shrink while capacity increases, some modelers have looked at electric power of ducted fans as a future possibility. Despite the power-to-weight disadvantages of electric motors and their batteries compared to equivalent glow engines and their fuel requirements, some consider the duct drag reduction and simpler installation requirements as benefits which might outweigh the disadvantages. Experiments continue but at this time an airframe-to-motor/battery ratio still demands a fifty-fifty share of the total weight.

The urge of some to go the ultimate route and provide a real gas turbine pressure jet engine has resulted in some interesting but not yet practical projects. The most noticeable to date is the Kavan turbojet engine introduced at the last Nuremberg Toy Fair. It is a centrifugal-flow jet which puts out fifty-five pounds of thrust yet weighs seventeen pounds, a power-to-weight ratio that doesn't compare favorably with the glow engine and ducted fan combination. The attendant complexities of the starter and fuel pump positions in relation to the engine itself would complicate the installation in a more conventional model. It brings the question of whether jet and scale jet models will be simplified to the point where they can be accessed by more modelers or whether they will evolve into the highly technical realm of a few elite modelers.

			Engine Specifications				
Engine	Displacement (ci)	Hp @ rpm	Compression ratio	Weight (oz.)	Width of crankcase (in.)	Carb position	Head
OS .25VF-DF	0.2485	1.10 @ 22,000	11.5:1	8.43	1.19	Front	Regular
OS .46VR-DF	0.455	1.9 @ 23,000	12.5:1	13.4		Rear	Regular
OS .77VR-DF	0.777	3.9 @ 23,000	12.5:1	22.22	1.65	Rear	Byron or regular
Rossi R65 RV-DF	0.6511	3.49 @ 21,000	10.5:1	27.1	1.72	Rear drum valve	Regular
Rossi .81RV-DF	0.81	4.7 @ 19,500	11.1:1	28.9	1.72	Rear drum valve	Byron or regular
K&B 3.5cc	0.21	.88 @ 22,000	13.5:1	6.8	1.16	Front	Regular
K&B 7.5cc	0.45	2.3 @ 22,500	14.5:1	13.2	1.34	Front	Regular
KBV .72	0.72	4.0 @ 23,000		22	1.745	Rear	Regular
Picco 80	0.81	5.0 @ 22,000		24	1.745	Rear	Byron
OPS Super SPP Fan	0.81	4.55 @ 21,000 (with 50% nitro)	ca. 13.5:1	22.2		Rear	Regular

Note: all piston liners are ABC style

Chapter 4

Aerodynamics and design

Full-size jet aircraft are designed for speed and altitude. These two factors governed a major change in the way aircraft were flown and how they looked. To the modelers striving to recreate these jet aircraft with fan units, it means creating and mastering new building techniques and learning how all those sleek lines such as swept wings, deltas or T-tails would translate into a flying scale model.

To model designers accustomed to the fundamental rule of thumb of mixing and matching, the new looks of jet aircraft meant incorporating additions to those basic rules. In one way, the basic layout work, as with any scale model, is already done. Modelers simply have to decide on the scale, estimate weights, areas and so on, and generally follow the scale outlines of the plane. But in many respects, because some of that layout was expressly intended for flight speeds in another world from model speeds, the pioneer model jet designers had to gauge the aerodynamic effects the new look of jets would have on their models.

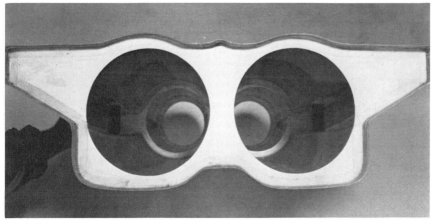

This is an internal bulkhead on a Byron F-15 and is typical of the internal structure of a fiberglass ducted-fan plane. The twin Byro-Jets mount in the bulkhead openings.

The primary consideration was aerodynamic. For example, the swept wing, one of the hallmarks of jet aviation, had to be understood. Its primary effects on models related to the center of gravity, its dihedral effect and the structural requirements of building this type of wing. Wing sweep gives a plane the same stabilizing effect as dihedral. For approximately every five degrees of sweep, the wing is the equivalent of one degree of dihedral. In this case, despite the fact that the primary reason for sweep was to help the wing fly without problems near the speed of sound, it worked to the advantage of the modeler.

What did become a problem was the location of the center of gravity (CG). To find its position meant locating the mean aerodynamic center and chord of the wing and its relative position on the fuselage. The mean aerodynamic center can be considered as the central position of the wing's area. The mean aerodynamic chord is the width of the wing at the mean aerodynamic center. If the modeler relied on the traditional method of establishing the CG between twenty-five and thirty percent of the wing chord or width at the fuselage and balanced the plane at that point, the CG position would be too far forward for the airplane to ever rotate its nose for takeoff. Guessing at the CG would put it too far to the rear, making the plane too pitch sensitive and possibly uncontrollable.

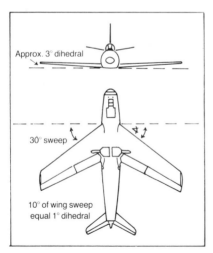

The dihedral effect of wing sweep is calculated by a simple formula: every five degrees of wing sweep from the perpendicular is equal to one degree dihedral. Thus, a wing with a 30-degree sweep has a dihedral of six degrees.

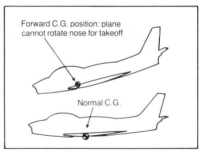

Placing the center of gravity point too far to the front of the plane results in an aircraft that cannot rotate its body for takeoff.

The structure of the swept wing also became a problem for conventional wood model techniques. On a straight wing of either constant chord or taper, the spar usually runs on a straight line through the center section of the wing tying the left and right wing panels together. The spar is conveniently located behind the center of gravity where the main landing gear ought to go. On a model's swept wing that's not possible. The two main spars can't be joined in a straight line and that means a weak center-section joint. The solution is a center cross-brace or secondary spar that ties the two wing panel spars together to form a rigid triangle. This brace spar must also be positioned to support the stress of the main landing gear.

That is one specific difference between ducted fans and more conventional propeller aircraft. There are more, and understanding the major ones helps both the designer and the modeler, because each must deal with them and their effects. Let's take a look at the major design trends used on full-size jet airplanes and their effect on model design and structure.

Planforms

One of the key words in the discussion of the design of a full-size jet is planform which refers to the outline shape of the wing and is determined by the job the plane must do. Faced with the increased complexity of high-speed flight and the fuel-guzzling jet engines, there are a variety of plan-

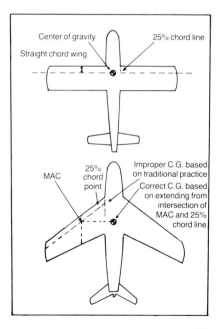

Proper placement of the center of gravity is critical. Finding the C.G. of a plane with straight wings is simple: draw a line showing 25 percent of the wing's chord from the front wing edge, and project a line directly across the fuselage to place the C.G. in the center of the body. Finding the C.G. on a swept-wing plane is more difficult. First, the point where the mean aerodynamic center (MAC) meets the 25 percent chord line must be found. Then the C.G. can be measured by extending from the intersection of the MAC and the 25 percent chord line to the center of the plane's fuselage.

79

forms. The early jets used conventional planforms with straight, usually tapered, wings. In some instances their low-thrust engines couldn't push them as fast as prop planes so they didn't need the complex variety of wing outline. Later fighters, which approached the sound barrier, and the more recent fighters, started to sprout swept wings, then deltas and then blended bodies.

The purpose of sweep on jets has already been discussed. Delta planforms were used where great strength and a large fuel-carrying load were required. The short span of the delta helped make it stronger. The internal structure of the wing could carry more fuel than on a conventional wing. Blended body structures were chosen to cut down the reflection of radar and help the plane become almost invisible. The structure also helped turn the fuselage of the plane into a lifting surface as well.

For any plane, model or full-size, these planforms have a definite effect on placing the CG in an uncharacteristic place, and on a point called center

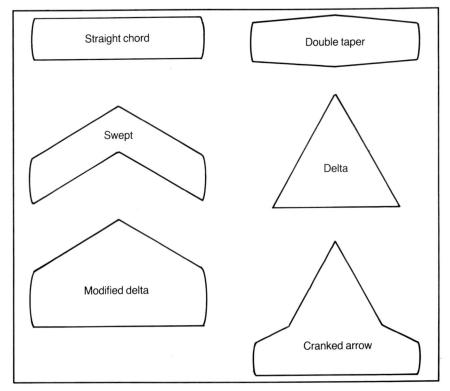

Wing planforms.

of pressure. A simplistic explanation of center of pressure (CP) states that it is the position along the span of the wing where the wing's lift is concentrated. It is always behind the center of gravity and it is not the same thing as the mean aerodynamic center. Every plane has a center of pressure and its position varies with the speed and the angle of attack on the plane. On straight-wing models the CP shift is not too great. On swept wings, it's a little moreso, but on a delta, it moves quite a bit.

The CP is caused by the airflow over the wings' surface. On wings with a lot of sweep, the flow drifts outward toward the tips. The greater the sweep, as is usually the case with a delta, the more the drift toward the tips. This outward drift cleans up the flow on the inboard section, increasing its share of the lifting load, and since the inboard section of a swept wing is closer to the nose, it moves the center of pressure forward.

If the CG on a delta is slightly off, there is the possibility that with the nose up at a high angle of attack, the CP shift might go forward of it. When that happens, the model pitches up suddenly and uncontrollably. A classic example would be slowing up a model with a delta wing on final for landing and raising the nose too high. If the CG was within the center of pressure

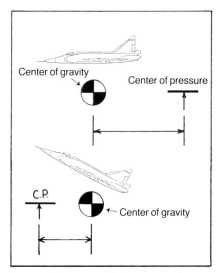

Proper placement of the center of pressure in regard to the center of gravity is also critical. If the C.P. shifts forward of the C.G., bottom, the result is an uncontrollable upward pitch. Ideally, the C.P. should shift behind the C.G. for stable flying, top.

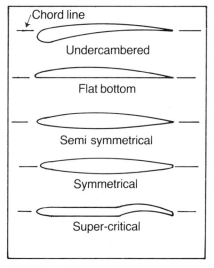

Airfoil profiles.

range, the pitch up would be sudden and severe. For that reason, on jet models prone to large center of pressure shifts, the center of gravity is usually placed so that it does not come close to the CP shift region.

Practically, this means that a model would be better off balanced nose-heavy. In this condition, the worst that could happen would be the inability of the model to rotate its nose for takeoff. In the other situation, the nose would rotate too easily and the model would pitch up uncontrollably. If it

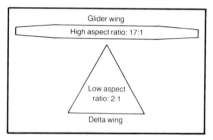

Aspect ratios differ radically between gliders and delta-winged jets, allowing the different craft to perform their different functions.

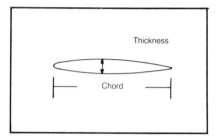

To find the thickness to chord ratio, the wing's thickness at its highest airfoil point is divided by the chord of the wing.

The first operational American jet, the F-80 Shooting Star, was a conventional airplane that used a jet engine instead of a prop and a reciprocating engine. It exhibited none of the performance or sophistication of later jets. Here are two ducted-fan models of the Shooting Star.

were able to successfully complete its takeoff, the remaining flight time would be a series of porpoising dives. In the modern planforms, such as the blended bodies like the SR-71 Blackbird or cranked arrow wings as on the F-16XL where the fuselage itself actually becomes a lifting body, the CG-CP relationship is even more complex.

The variety of jet planforms has an effect on two more important factors, aspect ratios and airfoils. Aspect ratio, which is the ratio of the wing-span squared to the wing area,

$$\text{Aspect Ratio (AR)} = \frac{\text{wing span}}{\text{mean chord}}$$

has a large effect on the drag produced by lift. On low aspect ratio wings like a delta, the drag is high. On high aspect ratio wings like a glider, the drag is low. Because of their speed and the loads imposed, jets went to lower aspect ratios as the structure needed to support a long wing would have been too heavy. To get around the drag problem, low aspect ratios use less effective lifting wings.

Airfoils

This brings us to the difference in airfoils or the side profile shape of the wing for full-size and model jets. Full-size gliders, using high-lift wings,

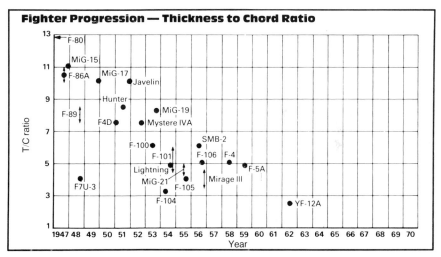

The progression of fighter planforms thickness to chord ratios. The general formula states that as performance and speed increase, the thickness to chord ratio decreases.

generally have undercambered profiles producing high lift. Most full-size propeller aircraft have used semisymmetrical or fully symmetrical wings. The same holds true for models.

Early full-size jets used the same airfoils as the high-speed propeller aircraft because their speeds were similar. As the jet speeds increased, the airfoils became more subtly shaped to deal with the special problems of flight beyond the sound barrier. To help kill lift and drag induced by the lower aspect ratios, the airfoils became thinner.

To express this thick and thin factor, a thickness-to-chord ratio is used which measures the thickness of the wing at the highest point of its curvature to the length of the wing chord at its root. On early full-size jets like the P-80 Shooting Star, the thickness at the highest point of curvature was approximately thirteen percent. From that point on, the thickness-to-chord ratio went down as speeds went up until it got to the lowest point with the F-104 Starfighter at a mere 3.36 percent.

To the model designer of a 1/9 scale Starfighter jet, a 3.36 percent thickness would come out to a wing no more than 1/2 inch thick at its high point. Such a wing is unacceptable for a model as it would not be strong enough nor would it have sufficient lifting capability. Consequently, the scale model jet designer must "fudge" the scale thickness and airfoil shape to satisfy the dual needs of strength and lifting capability.

Jets are designed for speed in the air so high-lift devices are required to allow them to fly slowly enough for realistic landing speeds. This F-104 Star-fighter model shows a leading edge flap and a trailing edge flap. Though models generally don't need this complexity, the wings on this plane are so thin that it really helps.

Some models use flying stabilizers. This shows the pivot rod on an F-18 Hornet model and the two retention screws which hold the stabilizer in place after it slides on the rod.

So far, the semisymmetrical airfoil has found favor as the best all-around choice for sufficient lift capability in model jets while also allowing good speed potential. This type of airfoil gets around the lifting characteristic of a flat-bottom airfoil which could present a problem for the higher speeds which model jets fly at. Flat-bottom airfoils get into problems when pitch trim changes compete with changes in speed. Symmetrical airfoils also offer a good alternate choice, but lack better lift characteristics.

Most conventional model planes have thickness ratios ranging from the average thirteen percent of sport model designs to the higher thicknesses of up to eighteen percent for trainer models and the new FAI pattern aircraft. To maintain the scale effect of jet models, the thickness ratio has to stay lower, averaging around nine to ten percent. In the case of the delta planform aircraft, with such wide root chords, the thickness ratio actually becomes less, usually about six to seven percent.

Coupled with the position on the wing chord where the greatest thickness or high point is, the ratio determines the lifting and speed capability. The higher the ratio, the greater the lift. The thinner the wing at the high point, the less the lift capability. The further forward the high point is, the greater the lift but the higher the drag. If the high point is moved back, there's less lift, but also less drag.

Model designers mix and match these general characteristics to get the proper blend for either a jet model designed for scale competition or for speed performance.

Control surfaces

Planform also affects control surfaces in full-size jets and has led in some instances to control surfaces that would be difficult to duplicate in a model. Let's look again at some of the planforms already discussed and see what sort of control surfaces have been employed and for what reasons.

Swept wings usually employ the tail plane with elevator for pitch control and ailerons for roll control. As speeds on full-size jets with swept wings increased, however, a problem called control divergence occurred. Ailerons are usually situated at the extreme outboard section of the wing trailing edge. Because the wing tips were tapered to a thinner profile and were less rigid, the aerodynamic forces on a deflected aileron could actually twist the wing in the opposite direction and reverse the direction of the control input and left aileron input could actually roll the plane right. Hence later swept-wing jets employed spoilers, control devices on the top of the wing located just past mid-span, to effect roll control.

On models, the same problem could exist if the tips are not rigid enough to resist the twisting which the ailerons could impart. Spoilers actuated one at a time are a possibility, but on a model give a more rapid roll rate and potential spin problems. The usual solution is to use nonscale but proven strip ailerons.

Delta planforms provide a special problem when it comes to control surfaces. Since there obviously is no tail in a pure delta, the control surfaces on the trailing edge must serve dual functions as both elevator for pitch and aileron for roll control.

On a model there are two ways to do this. The trailing edge control surface can be a single piece which functions as an elevon, a control surface which effects both roll and pitch control in a single surface. Such a surface requires some sort of mixing arrangement whether it be by mechanical means or a special feature on the transmitter.

The other method is the use of a split control surface. The trailing edge is divided between a surface used exclusively for pitch control (usually the

On this F-100 model, the high-lift de-vices are a large inboard trailing edge flap and a full-length leading slat.

Slats generally slide forward and sep-arate from the wing, while leading edge flaps are hinged and droop down.

surface closest to the fuselage) and a surface used exclusively for roll control (the outer surface). There is no possibility for flaps as they would only complicate the situation. Because a delta has no tail, there also would be no way to correct the pitch trim change which flaps create.

Another critical characteristic of a delta planform is called reflex, the upward curvature of the airfoil at the trailing edge. The reflex is tied to the center of pressure travel and helps tame the wide shift which deltas are prone to. It's not difficult to do and is as easy as trimming the trailing edge control surfaces up instead of remaining in a neutral position. Some airfoils have the reflex actually a part of the control surface profile.

Probably the most difficult control surface configuration for a modeler to cope with is variable geometry. This term refers to planes like the F-111 or F-14 Tomcat which can change the sweep of their wings to take advantage of the benefits of a variety of planforms. For the flight speeds which the modeler sees, variable geometry is of no practical benefit. As a triumph of modeling ingenuity it would be unequaled.

Depending on the sweep angle, a variable geometry wing can exploit the benefits of a delta for high-speed flight, or the low-speed benefits of a

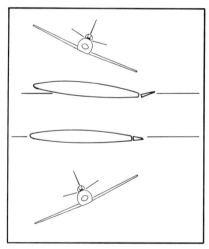

With an upward aileron deflection on the left wing, the plane is supposed to bank to the left. Aileron reversal occurs when the wing structure cannot resist the twisting imparted on it by the aileron, forcing the wing to twist upward. This increased angle of attack causes the plane to bank in the opposite direction, bottom.

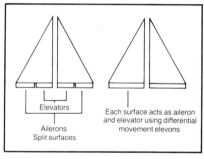

Delta wing control surfaces.

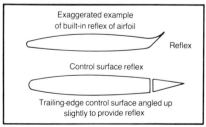

Reflex of delta airfoil.

One of the more widely used planforms is the delta, like that on Ivan Munninghoff's F-102. The trailing edge shows a single surface on either side which serves the dual function of aileron and elevator through differential movement. Above the tailpipe are operating split speed brakes.

The Saab AJ37 Viggen was the first jet to utilize the canard concept. On this Viggen model by Bob Thacker, the canards have a fixed forward surface (a stabilizer) and a hinged rear surface which function as flaps, not as pitch controllers.

high aspect ratio wing in a single airframe. But this means that conventional control surfaces like ailerons and elevator are impossible. Instead, the only means of pitch and roll control is through the tail surfaces. The horizontal stabilators act as both elevators for pitch control and ailerons for roll control. Duplicating an effective arrangement like this on a model is difficult, not because of the mixing required, but because of the amount of control-surface throw required. On a full-size F-14 Tomcat the amount of up and down movement of the stabilator elevons is considerably more than that of conventional control surfaces. Coupled to that is the fact that this control system is augmented by an on-board computer.

So far, two ducted-fan models of an F-14 have flown. One, designed by Jim Gupton, and modified by Bill Kolisko, used flaps and ailerons. The model's wings did sweep but not as much as the full sixty-eight-degree sweep of the full-size aircraft. Instead, Kolisko had the model's wings go from the full-forward sweep of twenty degrees back only to forty-eight degrees in flight. At that sweep, the ailerons were still effective but not scale. The flaps were deployed only when the wing was full-forward.

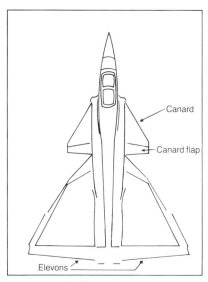

The canard planform, as seen on a Saab AJ37 Viggen.

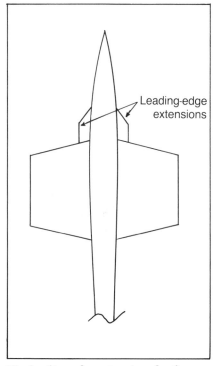

The leading edge extension planform.

89

The planform now in vogue is the canard, a horizontal flying surface which is positioned ahead of the wing and designed to act as an elevator, flap, or maneuvering device. It is usually coupled to a delta wing, and was first used on the Swedish Saab AJ37 Viggen. In this plane, the canard surface has a flap which was deployed at takeoff and landing to maintain a high angle of attack so the plane could fly slow enough to land or takeoff in a short distance.

The reason for swapping the tail lay in the canard's effective stall resistance. If properly designed, the canard will stall or lose its lift before the main wing. As the nose keeps trying to go up, the canard stalls, lets the nose drop, and flying speed is maintained. Note the words properly designed. A canard needs the proper amount of aerodynamic loading which is achieved by its area. Too small an area and the nose cannot come up. Too large an area and the nose can't stop going up. Again, for the scale modeler most of the calculating is taken out by the dimensions incorporated in the full-size plane being modeled.

In a canard, the CG is at a point well forward of the wing and is determined by the aerodynamic centers of both the canard surface and the main wing plus the ratio of lift each wing provides. The calculations are complex and one of the best explanations was offered by Col. Robert Thacker in the article he did for his radio-controlled model of the Saab Viggen in the July 1986 issue of *Scale R/C Modeler.*

This F-16XL model built by Ivan Munninghoff shows the cranked arrow planform. The trailing edge is split into a conventional elevator (inboard) *and aileron (outboard). The F-16 uses what is called a chin inlet. Ivan Munninghoff*

Important to note in a canard is the direction of movement in control surfaces to give pitch up or down. On a conventional tail, the upward movement of the elevator gives a nose pitch up. On a canard, the same upward movement gives the exact opposite effect, a nose pitch down. In some instances, the canards are coupled to the elevon or elevator movement of the main delta wing. As the elevator or elevon is deflected upward for pitch up, the canard is deflected downward. The amount of travel is determined by a trial-and-error process.

There are more planforms being experimented with for full-size jet aircraft, each an attempt to address aerodynamic problems arising from mission requirements. LERX, MAW, CCV and FSW are four such experiments and mention is made of them to explain that planform of any airplane is a compromise of advantage and disadvantage.

LERX is an acronym for leading-edge root extension, denoting an extra area added forward of the wing's leading edge in the root area to improve lift on the inboard section of the wing. It was added to the full-size F-20 Tigershark and has already been tried on a model as a modification of Matt Snell's Jet Model Products Starfire, a successful attempt to cope with the problem of a 6,800 foot altitude at his model-flying site.

MAW is an acronym for mission adaptive wing, referring to present experiments with an F-111 to actually change the camber or curvature of the

Robert Oliveira's futuristic model design follows the trends of advanced fighter planform. It shows what's called a blended body, where the fuselage and wing blend into one shape instead of distinct geometries. At the *nose are canards in what is known as CCV configuration. Surfaces like these can move differentially to make the fighter perform unheard-of sidestepping or vertical elevator-like climbs.*

wing to provide the best lift ability of the wing for a specific phase of flight. Unlike leading-edge or trailing-edge flaps which usually extend the area of a wing and are positioned to exact locations, MAW wings actually bend to almost any shape. The full-size MAW technology is still new and still too unproven to utilize in a model.

CCV can be translated as control-configured vehicle, describing the addition of extra control surfaces to airframes to leapfrog their maneuverability to unheard-of capability. For example, a CCV-configured F-16 Falcon would be capable of sidestepping, a lateral move ninety degrees to its flight path. So far, like the MAW, the technology is still too new and unproven to incorporate in models, but once the basic factors are defined and given numbers, this design concept may show up in models.

FSW is a new concept that reverses the old swept wing concept by aiming the wings forward. Although the only aircraft to use this concept to date, the Grumman X-29, is highly unstable, it is not due to the forward sweep. The wing is actually more stable at a high angle of attack, like that in a landing approach, than a conventional rear swept wing because the airflow over the FSW wing follows the chord more than the traditional sweep planform. At a high angle of attack the flow tends to curve over the rear sweep wing along the span of the wing rather than over the chord.

To date three models have been known to fly successfully with FSW. One was a ducted-fan proof-of-concept aircraft based on the X-29. Two others were R/C model propeller aircraft. One, the FSW-3, designed by Don Sobbe and published in the February 1987 issue of *Radio Control Modeler,* had an FSW with constant chord, no taper and a wood frame which flew quite well. To provide the required stiffness at the wing tips, the open bay sections were sheeted with 1/16 balsa like the center section.

Designed by Tom Hunt, this small ducted-fan model of the Grumman X-29 shows a forward swept wing. This particular planform is quite efficient but could not be economically and structurally realized until the advent of the new composite materials.

Individual designs

To the designer of a scratchbuilt ducted-fan plane, many of the considerations which full-size designers must deal with are meaningless. Some of the complex increased-lift control surfaces such as leading-edge flaps or trailing-edge flaps are simply not necessary to help the plane fly and in some instances may actually make it uncontrollable. For example, Ivan Munninghoff designed a Byro-Jet-powered F-16XL based on the Byron Originals F-16 kit. The XL version of the F-16 used a delta planform instead of the original wing-tail planform. The full-size plane had leading-edge flaps to augment lift at takeoff. Munninghoff tried to duplicate these devices on the model XL and quickly found that the flaps had to be totally symmetrical in operation. If one retracted slightly faster, the asymmetrical configuration would roll the plane. Locking the flaps in position, he found that the model took off just as well.

Model jet designers have realized that outside of accounting for the aerodynamic peculiarities of jet planforms, their primary design challenge is to make a model from the inside out and to provide a strong structure for that planform. Typical model structures many times don't suffice because of the complex compound curvatures of some scale jets. T-tails, mid-wings, fuselage-mounted gear, podded engines and so on are new structural problems to model designers. Light weight, most critical in jets, must be main-

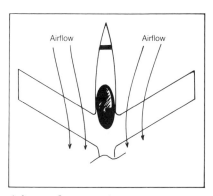

A forward-swept wing.

Another of the experiments being tried today is thrust vectoring which diverts the thrust from a jet up or down or sideways, to change the attitude of the aircraft or help it rotate more quickly to shorten takeoff. This model of Tom Hunt's 2001 shows the pitch vector vane between the two tails. Tom Hunt

tained but some of these structures demand heavy materials to provide sufficient strength.

So far, the emphasis has been on scale jet aircraft and that's where the primary direction of ducted-fan models has gone. Meanwhile, a new class of fan models has emerged, the performance fans, which place an emphasis on speed. These planes share some of the structural requirements of the scale jets but their designers have the liberty of choosing profiles that suit their own goals. Scale modelers have always been plagued by fidelity to the outlines of the aircraft they intend to model. Sometimes that fidelity works fine and the model can easily be reproduced. Sometimes it doesn't. In scale jet models there has always been a major stumbling block that has governed the suitability of a scale subject and it has to do with the tailpipe diameter.

This dimension, on a full-size aircraft, is governed by the type of jet engine used. In the early years of jet flight, there were two basic kinds, the centrifugal flow and the axial flow. Both were true turbojets, engines that relied on compressing air to a high pressure. Because they were low power, the nozzles were small to keep the velocity and pressure of the jet thrust sufficiently powerful. The centrifugal-flow engines had a high ratio of engine diameter size to nozzle diameter size. Compare the wide fuselage diameter of the F-80 Shooting Star to its small nozzle diameter. Many of the early jets shared this design.

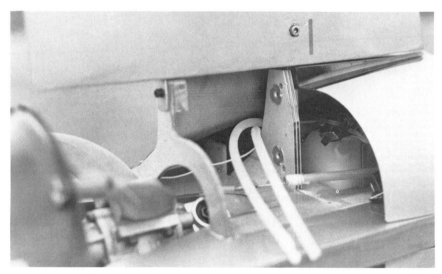

Adequate structure can become a problem because the geometries of jets don't cooperate with traditional modeling structural techniques. This picture shows the fore and aft spar attach points on a Sterner SportFAN. Load paths must be considered carefully and materials chosen wisely.

To the scale jet designer this becomes a problem. Ratios of shroud diameter to tailpipe diameter are lower. This means that if the ratios are not close enough, either the tailpipe must be enlarged to accommodate the fan unit chosen—which may alter the looks of the plane—or the fuselage must be scaled up to accommodate the tailpipe nozzle diameter that works best with the fan unit. Both are no-win situations and this becomes perhaps the biggest determining factor of a plane's suitability to a jet model designer. If he or she chooses the non-scale tailpipe, it may alter the scale looks sufficiently to detract from the appearance of the jet. If he or she decides in favor of the scale nozzle diameter, then the fuselage may have to be blown up to a size and weight beyond the thrust capability of the fan unit.

The group of model jet designers active today has evolved some ingenious ways of coping with all these factors and producing aircraft that fly—and fly well. No longer do they have to deal with insufficient power and, sharing their experience with one another, they have accumulated some design details which are instructive for all those who want to model a ducted-fan aircraft. Most of them are not engineers; all of them are dedicated to expanding the scope of ducted-fan modeling to a level where it's viable for any modeler.

The best way to eliminate flutter, especially on all-moving surfaces like this F-15 stabilizer, is to keep pushrods short and rigid. The surface pivot is about mid-span, while the horn is near the leading edge, another way of dampening flutter with the actuating point as far as possible from the pivot point.

Chapter 5

Materials and building

The consequence of the full-size jet aircraft's high speed is the necessity of streamlined shapes. For the early ducted-fan modelers who were scale oriented, the jet's complex shapes presented a problem. First, fuselage shapes became sleeker to cut down on drag, and when the dramatic effects of the sound barrier emerged as a daily dilemma, the shapes became even more radical. Compound curvatures were the norm; a straight line in a plane became an oasis in a desert of subtle but beautiful geometries.

Swept wings became common to deal with stability at high speed and the sound barrier. The spar structure to support such a wing became a more complex and weightier task. Wing thicknesses shrunk, again to minimize drag at high speed. Landing gear found unconventional places to nest and complex rotation geometries to get there. The essential inlets were novel and complex factors.

Materials came to be an important consideration. Relying on the strength of the same materials in conventional aircraft to accomplish these new tasks was unacceptable and carried heavy weight penalties. Creation of new and high-strength, lightweight materials became a major need.

The same materials problem confronts the ducted-fan modeler. The shapes of modern jet aircraft made the modeler's traditional reliance on an all-wood structure almost obsolete. To achieve the strength required in reproducing the shape of the jet aircraft meant an increase in the parts count and complexity of the framework. Consider the fuselage of the Grumman F9F-8 Cougar as an example. The wing fuselage juncture of this plane is an intricate design; for a modeler to create a wooden substructure from traditional balsa with sufficient strength would be laborious.

To the ducted-fan modelers of the fifties and sixties, complexity was a way of life because balsa was the only suitably light material available. Their models were a dazzling blend of craftsmanship and ingenuity inspired by their desire to create models light enough to fly with minimal amounts of thrust. Every sliver of wood, every glue joint, every ounce of covering skin had to be carefully assessed for its weight. Internal structure had to be evaluated for its contribution to authenticity, strength and, again, light weight.

Today we're blessed with abundant thrust, miracle materials and refined applications. The challenge which ducted-fan modelers have now is the intelligent choice of a wide variety of strong, but lightweight materials.

Glass fiber, foam, carbon fiber, Kevlar, pressure-impregnated materials and balsa, along with cyanoacrylates, epoxies, polyester resins, casting and molding materials, plastics and paint finishes are available for those who want to scratchbuild a plane or assemble a commercial kit. For the kit builder most of the selection process is done, but some of the materials can be used to selectively reinforce or modify the model. For the scratchbuilder there are many options of material and construction for any purpose.

Fiberglass

The material which has saved ducted-fan modelers the weight buildup in complex jet structures is fiberglass-reinforced resins, known simply as fiberglass. A blend of fiberglass cloth and epoxy or polyester resins, it was first used in aerobatic pattern aircraft in the mid-seventies and quickly adopted for the scale jet aircraft being designed for the Turbax and Byron fans. Fiberglass gives a model an almost instant external shell that can retain its shape with few internal bulkheads. The layup, or process of creating a fiberglass fuselage, bypasses all the laborious steps required to build a conventional wooden frame structure, such as cutting individual parts, alignment of the framework, gluing it together and putting a rigid skin over it. With an accurate mold and proper layup techniques, a straight, strong fiberglass fuselage can be constructed in a few hours, allowed to cure for a day or two, and be ready for equipment installation long before an equivalent wooden airframe would be.

It is the combination of properties that recommends the fiberglass technique. A fuselage the size of a radio-control plane could be cast from either

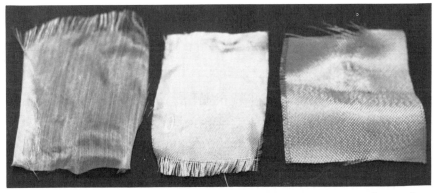

Fiberglass cloth comes in different weights measured in ounces per square yard. From left to right: the ultrafine 0.60 ounce cloth for fine surface finish; the common 2.0 ounce cloth used for reinforcement and sometimes mold buildup; and the coarser weave of the 6.0 ounce cloth used to quickly build up molds or fuselages.

the polyester or the epoxy resin, just like a plastic model airplane. These resins are two-part liquids, one of which is the actual resin and the other a catalyst which hardens or cures the resin to a plastic after it is added. Because the resin lacks strength and is brittle, the necessary thickness to give it strength and resist cracking would make it absurdly heavy and the skin of the model would have to be almost an inch thick. Resin is liquid, however, and can conform to any shape after it is hardened with a catalyst.

Fiberglass cloth is strong and light. It is actually fine strands of real glass woven into fabrics in varying thicknesses for different applications. By itself, it is extremely tear resistant. In the lighter cloths used in ducted-fan and other planes, it can be draped and pressed in place to follow almost any contour. The resin is needed to hold and set the cloth in place. Of all the adhesives which could be used, the epoxy or polyester resins have the best body and strength to give the fiberglass-resin combination sufficient rigidity.

Selection of the proper cloth and resin are based on certain needs. Let's take the cloth first. The weave of the cloth is important and almost all modeling applications use the bidirectional weave, which means that the glass fibers are woven into a perpendicular crisscross pattern. This gives strength in two directions instead of one, as in unidirectional fiberglass cloth which has the bulk of its strands running parallel with smaller strands crisscrossing them to hold the fibers together.

Cloth weight is another important consideration. Fiberglass is measured in ounces per square foot, and in modeling applications runs from a mere 0.6 ounce per square foot up to about eight ounces per square foot. A fiberglass fuselage is constructed of a combination of weights and layers to satisfy the individual or manufacturer. The fine weave of the lighter glass cloths is usually the layer which goes on the surface of the fuselage because the resin easily fills the pores between the strands and gives a smooth, even surface. The heavier-weight glass cloths go under the thin outer layer to add strength. These strength layers can be single or double depending on the complexity of contours and the required weight. If the fuselage has relatively simple contours without sharp corners and bulges, a single layer of six-ounce cloth might be used to back up the outer layer. If weight or contour changes are part of the fuselage, a lighter cloth may be selected to drape more easily into the fuselage contours requiring less resin to fill the smaller pores.

There are also resin requirements, whether they be epoxy or polyester. Besides the strength already mentioned, they must first of all be low viscosity, or thin, since resins come in all degrees of thickness. Low-viscosity resins, usually referred to as laminating resins, are like a syrup. The resins used for gluing are usually high viscosity and thicker, sometimes as thick as dough. A good laminating resin has the proper blend of strength with sufficient thinness so that it can penetrate the glass completely and adhere it to the other layers providing a smooth surface.

Both the polyester resin and the epoxy resin are two-part catalyzed resins. That simply means that they both harden after a catalyst is added to start the hardening reaction, or cure. The choice between polyester and epoxy is one of preference based on cost, working environment and health factors. Epoxy is regarded as the stronger of the two resins and it does not shrink when it cures. To maintain the proper viscosity and a reasonable curing time, however, epoxy must be used in a narrow temperature range or it gets too thick. Some people have allergic reactions to the epoxy, and it is the costlier of the two.

Polyester resins are less expensive, retain their low viscosity over a wider temperature range and can yield a finer finish. But they have their disadvantages, too. First of all, they will not cure over all kinds of epoxy and are not compatible when used with other materials. They also have a slight shrinkage factor during cure, and the catalyst used with them can cause irreversible damage if it gets in your eye.

There is another factor in working successfully with the glass called sizing, a term which refers to a special chemical treatment of the glass cloth. Part of the success of the glass-resin combination depends on the ability of the resin to completely soak the cloth's woven strands. This is why viscosity is so important; if the resin is too thick, it will drag the cloth away from its position, weakening the whole structure. The sizing wicks the resin all around the glass strands, provided the resin's viscosity is suitably low. The trade name for one sizing is Volan A, and it is the sizing agent seen most often on fiberglass used in hobby applications.

Molds and plugs

A fiberglass fuselage needs something to define its shape while the resin is applied to the cloth and the fiberglass-resin mix cures. To define the shape, either a plug or a mold is needed; the choice is based on the number of fuselages desired and the ease of producing them.

A plug is the exact shape and size of the structure to be reproduced, whether it's a fuselage, an engine nacelle or a small hatch cover. It's usually a solid piece of material and once the plug has been shaped exactly, the fiberglass cloth can be laid directly over the plug and the resin applied. Of course, there has to be a way of getting the inside shape out once the fiberglass skin has cured. This usually requires the destruction of the plug, especially in the case of a fuselage. It also means that usually only a single part can be constructed from that plug.

A mold is used when a number of fuselages are required, and it is nothing more than a female image of the male plug. In this case the plug is not destroyed. It's used to shape the mold and then the fiberglass is laid into the female mold with the resin. Once cured, the fiberglass is popped out of the mold and the mold re-used.

Since fiberglass molding is such an important part of ducted-fan modeling, some familiarity with the techniques of making plugs and molds may be necessary. The process is not difficult, but is time-consuming. The secret is in using the proper materials.

The plug is the most difficult piece because it needs an accurate, true shape. The external finish must be clean, especially when used to make a female mold which will reproduce even the slightest imperfection. All sorts of materials have been used to make a plug, some expensive, some not.

For extreme accuracy, a plug can be made from architect's engineering foam. This is a high-density urethane foam that comes in weights from two up to twenty pounds per cubic foot. It is a granular-type foam which can be carved or sanded into detailed shapes. Its texture is similar to the green foam blocks that florists use for floral displays. The florist's foam is lighter

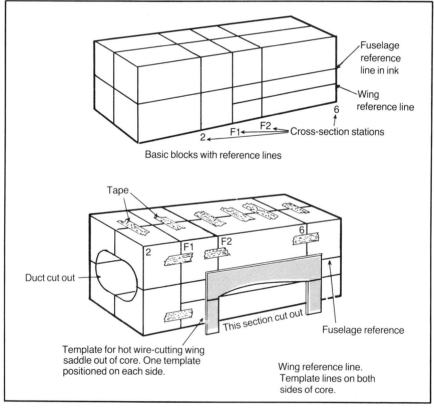

This illustration shows the method of making a one-time plug from foam blocks. Reference lines are drawn and templates aligned on them to make necessary cuts. When the plug is finished, it's covered with fiberglass and the internal foam core is melted or gouged out.

100

than structural foam, but is too light to stand much abuse. In model-making applications, a six- to ten-pound-per-cubic-foot density is sufficient, and the foam can be purchased in billets, or large blocks, in varying thicknesses and widths up to eight feet long. The chief drawback is expense. For example, a six-pound-per-cubic-foot billet measuring eight by twenty-four by ninety-six inches costs more than $300. Those using this type of foam for a plug generally build a wooden box structure to take up most of the volume of the shape and then put thick sheets of foam around this core structure, carving the external foam to shape.

Other plug materials are the white expanded-bead polystyrene foam most people refer to as Styrofoam. It too comes in different densities but is most commonly available in a two-pound-per-cubic-inch weight. Although it doesn't carve and sand nearly as easily as the architect's urethane foam, it is less costly and available in building supply stores in the form of wall insulation sheets.

If the plug will be destroyed after one fuselage is made, then it must be constructed of a solid or near solid piece of foam since there is no way to pry a rigid core box out of the interior of the fuselage. The most common method for a one-shot plug is to sandwich blocks of foam between internal formers in the fuselage, such as bulkheads for ducted-fan mounting, landing gear mounts, wing attachment and so on, and then carefully carve the plug to shape. After the fiberglass has been laid over the plug and cured, the inter-

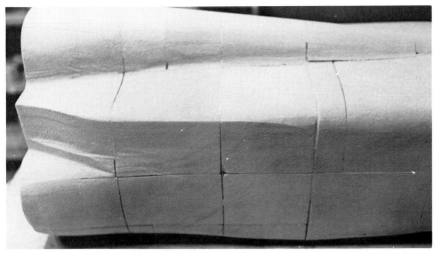

Urethane foam finds its use as the core material for plugs. Shown here is the plug for an F-18 Hornet being gradually shaped. Each of the lines shows a "station," *or cross section. Urethane foam is very granular and in the heavier densities, very expensive.*

nal foam is gouged out. Some modelers have poured gasoline inside the fuselage and dissolved the foam. This may be easier but it is potentially dangerous because of the toxic gases released. A little extra effort in this case will not hurt you.

If the plug will be used to make a female mold, there must be two mold halves, a right and a left. There is no other way of slipping the fuselage plug with all its contours and shapes from out of a single one-piece mold. Some people prefer to build a right- and a left-hand plug to make the respective molds. This method presents accuracy and alignment problems when it comes to joining the fuselage halves. For the extra time involved, it is more accurate to use the single plug and a parting board to make the two mold halves.

In either case, more fiberglass and resin materials are used. First of all the surface of the mold must be completely smooth. Any minor imperfections are filled with a resin paste and filler. The traditional spackling compound is not suitable on the outer surface because it can crack or tear easily. Once the surface is smooth and has the proper details, it must be waxed to prevent the gel coat from adhering to the plug. Next, a parting line is drawn down the top and bottom centerline of the fuselage plug. This parting line is a reference point for the parting board, which is usually a large single sheet of 1/4 or 1/2 inch plywood with the profile of the fuselage cut out. The parting board must be absolutely straight and match the parting line exactly, otherwise there will be voids in the fuselage centerline.

A template is sandwiched in the foam at each of the stations, and the fuselage cut and sanded to its outline. The perpendicular lines are fuselage reference centerlines.

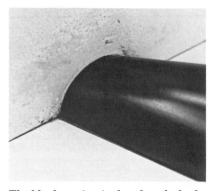

The black section is the aft end of a fuselage plug placed in what's known as a parting board. The parting board defines one half of the fiberglass part. A single full plug is preferred over half plugs because the full plug produces a much more accurate half mold than two separate plugs.

The plug is then inserted in the profile cutout of the parting board and the parting line on the plug matched exactly to the straight surface of the parting board. The plug is held in place and a simple modeling clay is inserted in the minor gap between the plug surface and the parting board. Once the clay has been blended to the surface of the plug and a slight radius given to the corner formed by the plug-parting board intersection, it's time to spray or brush a coat of mold release agent on the plug. This is usually a chemical called PVA which is alcohol-based, and forms a thin barrier between the plug and the first layer of the mold's fiberglass. The plug must be examined to make sure the PVA coverage is complete. If not, part of the skin of either the mold or the plug will be torn out.

Several different fiberglass materials are used to build up the mold to a thick, strong, rigid structure. The process is timely, but most of the effort is in simply letting the different layers of the mold cure. To get a smooth inside surface for the mold, a gel coat is sprayed on the plug over the PVA. This gel coat is a two-part resin that can form a tough, thin skin which flows out and takes the shape of even the most minute detail of the plug—including defects.

Once the gel coat has cured (two can be applied), successive layers of two- to six-ounce glass cloth are resined onto the plug half and parting board using a small stiff bristle brush to push the resin into the cloth weave and down to the preceding layer. After two or three layers of this heavier cloth, another type of fiberglass cloth is applied to build up the bulk of the mold. This cloth is called mat cloth and is made of random short fibers running in

Every detail must be carefully built into the plug, such as the windows on the fuselage plug of this Lear 35.

The fit of the fiberglass part to the mold is so tight that it must actually be pried from the mold. Special plastic wedges are used so the inner mold surface won't be damaged.

all directions with a special sizing agent to let the resin wick into the cloth. The female mold is complete when it is 1/4 to 1/2 inch thick.

One of the most important steps in constructing the mold is the drilling of the registration holes around the perimeter of the mold's lip to be used for aligning the two mold halves when joining the fuselage. When you try this, you'll see why the molds need to be so rigid; popping them off of the plug actually requires wedges made from wood or plastic so as not to damage the mold surface.

Using the mold method of construction means that you build the fuselage from the outside in. First, a liberal coat of PVA is sprayed on the inside surface of the mold so that the outside surface of the fuselage lamination does not stick. Next, a light cloth—some use even 3/4 ounce cloth—is laid into the mold, and then the resin is carefully brushed on in an even application. Lumps or puddles of resin add weight, and can leave weak spots in the fuselage. The light cloth is used to drape and cling to the details in the mold. A second light layer may be added after the first cures, and then a heavier layer, four to six ounce, used after that. This heavier layer becomes the inside surface of the fuselage and has a rough texture because of the bulkier weave of the cloth. One variation to this method of fuselage layup is to spray a thin gel coat into the mold to take the place of the first light glass cloth.

It should be apparent by now that fiberglass construction is not difficult. The challenge is in learning the idiosyncrasies of the resins and characteristics of the cloth. For example, how much resin must be mixed and how long can it be used? This question can be answered by the rule of thumb, mix small batches at a time, especially when using polyester resins which have a much shorter pot life, or working time, than epoxies. Another quirk of resins is that their cure time accelerates if they are in a small container

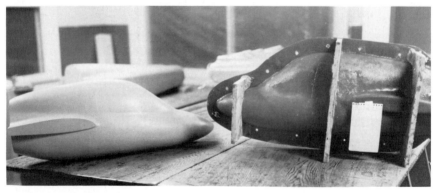

At left is the SportFAN plug which shaped the SportFAN mold at the right. When the molds wear out, the surface is periodically repaired with special resins.

with a minimal surface area. This kind of accelerated reaction generates heat and the hardening resin actually crackles and spits. Use a container that allows more surface area than depth.

This is a basic introduction to fiberglass work. Using this material means thinking ahead, having everything ready when you need it or you'll spend a lot of money on wasted materials. Unlike wood, you cannot go back and fix a delaminated mold or fuselage part. You have already seriously weakened a structure that relies on its total integrity for its rigidity and strength.

There are all sorts of variations on this technology. For instance, some people prefer to make their molds from plaster castings of the plug. It is less expensive than a resin-fiberglass mold but its disadvantage is that an extraordinary weight is needed to achieve the same rigidity and strength. It is also more prone to cracking and the inside surface of the mold is given to chipping.

Fuselage preparation

Many jet models use fiberglass fuselages, and many times this may be the modeler's first experience with this type of construction. There isn't the usual need to fill and sand as there is with a wood model to prepare the surface for paint or plastic finish. Still, to work with fiberglass there are a few things which must be done.

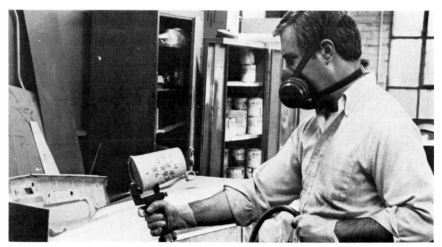

With the plug ready, Mark Frankel sprays the first gel coat on the plug. This gel coat is like a thin liquid plastic that forms the actual surface of the female mold. It reproduces the finest detail of the plug, even the imperfections like scratches, dust and so on. Note the respirator mask, a prudent and necessary precaution.

First, the surface should be protected as much as possible. Foam rubber or Styrofoam insulation sheet laid on the workbench prevents needless scratches and cracks from rough handling or equipment lying around.

Second, before any work is done on the fuselage, it should be cleaned. Some fuselages retain a film of mold release agent that could ruin a paint finish. Isopropyl alcohol or denatured alcohol (which can be purchased in paint supply stores) make inexpensive cleaning agents to remove the mold release. Soak a rag in the alcohol and rub it on the fuselage. Any mold release will crumble into rubbery bits and pieces as long as the rag is well-soaked. Do the entire fuselage at least twice and don't skimp on the alcohol. Those who demand the best finishes use automotive surface preparation cleaners like DuPont's Prep-Sol as they are designed to leave no film behind. They will also dissolve any grease or wax that also may have gotten on the fuselage. One caution: Use solvents with plenty of fresh air or with a respirator mask designed specifically for vapors.

Fiberglass must be treated like thin sheet metal when working with it and the same tools used for metal-working can be used for fiberglass. Cutting tools with coarse teeth catch and crack fiberglass. Fiberglass can be filed with a metal file quite well and cuts nicely with extremely fine-toothed saws or the Dremel silicone carbide cut-off wheels used for cutting music wire. 3M Open Coat or the Wetodry Tri-M-Ite automotive finishing sandpaper can be used when sanding. For cutting small curves or intricate lines, a jeweler's saw blade worked back and forth is accurate and leaves little kerf, or opening, where it has sawn.

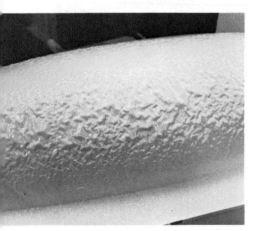

Any impurity in the gel coat can cause problems. This gel coat crinkled because too much styrene thinner was added to the gel coat mix.

This special gauge checks the thickness of the wet gel coat without leaving any marks. It measures in mils and is necessary to make sure there are no thin spots in the gel coat.

Working with fiberglass does not demand specialized tools, only specific tools for specific tasks. X-ACTO produces some fine-tooth saw blades for use with the different X-ACTO handles. The #39 and #34 razor saw blades can be used with the #5 handle for cutting straight lines. The #15 keyhole saw blade for the #5 handle has fine enough teeth to cut fiberglass. The #27 saw blade, used with a #2 handle, has even finer teeth and is much thinner, leaving a thinner kerf. For cutting around a small radius, the X-ACTO jeweler's saw blade, #43R, is perfect because of the fine kerf and tooth pattern on the blade. It's not necessary to use the saw handle with these blades. They can be held in both hands and simply worked back and forth. Try to maintain as much tension as possible and avoid flexing.

Dremel also has a number of versatile cutting tools which are used with its electric Moto-tools. As a general rule of thumb, any of the fine-grain aluminum oxide (#941, 997, 945, 952, 953, 954) or silicon carbide (#83142, 83322, 83702, 84642, 84922) grinding stones are good for working with the fiberglass. The high-speed and the carbide cutters have a tendency to chatter or grab the glass and can crack it.

Dremel also has some sanding drums (#408, 432) in different grits. Always choose the finest grit since it avoids the grabbing tendency of coarser grits or teeth. The same is a consideration when choosing the steel saws which Dremel makes (#400 and 406). The #400 is much finer and thinner than the #406. Silicon carbide cutting discs (#409, 420, 426) also work well.

Kerry Sterner, left, and Mark Frankel, right, begin draping two-ounce glass cloth over the cured gel coat on the plug. Successive layers of two- and six-ounce cloth are added until the mold is rigid, thick and strong.

The numbers reflect the three thicknesses of these wheels which are the ones used for cutting music wire.

In any sawing or sanding operations with fiberglass, wear a dust filter mask like those sold by 3M. The minute particles of glass resin dust don't break down with the passage of time like balsa dust might, and can remain in the respiratory tract, nasal passages and lungs for the rest of your life.

Since it's impossible to mold a fuselage in one piece, the two halves must be joined, which results in a center seam line. Working the raised lip of the seam down to the surface should be done carefully. A metal file or a rigid sanding block with 80 or 100 grit Production Paper can be used to level the seam, sanding from the low to the high side of the seam on a diagonal, using as little pressure as possible. Bearing down on the sandpaper to try to get it to do more work, more quickly actually depresses the seam below the surrounding surface because the fiberglass is flexible.

Some prefer to sand the seam level to the surface and then fill in the fine scratch marks with primer. Others prefer to abrade the gross seam ridge just about down to the surface and then butter on a slurry mix of microbal-

As the mold is built up, alignment holes are keyed in, a very necessary technique when joining the two fiberglass pieces in the mold. At this point, the fiberglass parts have not been released from the mold. Note the heavy reinforcement and the thickness of the mold, all required because of the stresses put on it.

loons and epoxy, Sig Epoxolite, or automotive polyester filler against the ridge of the seam. They then smooth this slurry with sanding. Some of the fuselages may have small voids, especially in the corners, where a small bubble of air was trapped when laying in the first layer of glass. These should be filled along with the seam lines and sanded smooth.

It is not advisable to use spackling compound as a filler. Even though it is light, it does not adhere as well to the smoother surface of fiberglass as it does to wood, and the vibration levels of the fans make it crack and flake off easily.

For sandpaper, Wetodry Tri-M-Ite is a fine-grained oxide paper and can be purchased almost anywhere hardware items or finishing materials are sold. The most common grits range from the relatively coarse 80 grit to fine 600 grit. Finer grits, used only during the paint finishing process, are available from automotive finishing stores. Tri-M-Ite paper also comes in what is called the Fre-Cut style. This can also be used but it has a tendency to quickly lose its grit. The Fre-Cut paper is a light grayish-white. The Wetodry is black and in the initial finishing stages, it should be used dry. Open Coat Production sandpaper is more readily available at hardware stores and comes in grits from 50 to 150. For fiberglass, the 80 and 100 grits are the most useful.

Besides the microballoon-epoxy slurry or Sig Epoxolite, several companies offer an epoxy filling mix which is suitable for carving or sanding. Model Magic Products offers Epoxy Plus and Penn International Chemicals offers Poxy Lite. Both are sandable two-part epoxies which are pre-loaded with microballoons.

Automotive stores sell the polyester filler putty used primarily for filling gaps in auto body repair. It is a two-part mixture consisting of the bulky filler material and a minute bead of the cream hardener catalyst. The original filler was heavy and had to be used sparingly on the fiberglass airframes. But its quick curing time of fifteen minutes and easy sanding recommend it where speed is essential.

The filler material offers choices depending on the need. Some fillers are the traditional kind with clay as the material which gives substance to the filler. A slightly less heavy filler, politely known as Gorilla Hair, is embedded with chopped glass fibers and strands, and is intended for strength. Some polyester filler is much lighter, consisting of microballoons. It is intended for simply filling voids. Whatever your choice of material, it must be based on its purpose. In simple filling operations, the microballoon filler is fine.

When drilling fiberglass, ordinary drill bits can be used safely up to about 1/8 inch diameter. Larger drill bits, especially 1/4 inch and up, can grab like a coarse-tooth cutter and crack or chip the fuselage. There are two solutions to this problem. One is to grind a sharper fifty-five-degree rake angle on any drill bits used with the fiberglass just as when drilling plexiglass. The other solution is to drill a small, centered pilot hole and enlarge it with one of Dremel's grinding stones. The #941 aluminum oxide stone does well for larger holes since it's shaped like a cone and can enlarge a pilot hole anywhere from the pilot hole diameter up to the stone's maximum 5/8 inch diameter. Larger holes can be ground out carefully by scribing the circumference of the hole and grinding to its outlines.

Foam

Fiberglass was one of the earliest of the miracle materials which have become known as composites because they blend two dissimilar materials into a better material than could be obtained in traditional ways. The chief advantage of composites is their strength-to-weight ratio and their ease of use in construction.

Expanded-bead foam wing cores have become one of the most widely used of composite materials in all parts of radio-control model aviation. In one piece they provide the shape of the wing, and are easily strengthened with an exterior sheeting of a 1/16 inch balsa wood skin. This can be sheeted with an ultralight glass cloth for a strong, smooth surface, or with a heat-shrinkable precolored plastic film.

Cutting the shape of the core requires a hot wire and templates. This hot wire is a length of nichrome wire attached to a cutting bow. Since the nichrome wire has a high resistance, an electric current passing through it heats the wire enough to melt the foam. To cut the core, a rectangular block of foam is first cut which has the area and thickness dimensions of the wing. Reference centerlines are drawn on the wing core and the stiff plywood or sheet aluminum templates of the wing center section side profile and the

Urethane foam, left, and polystyrene foam, right, require different working techniques and have distinct applications. Urethane works like soft balsa and comes in densities from 2 to 20 pounds per square inch. It can be cut and sanded like wood with regular woodworking tools, although it is too heavy to be used as a structural component. Polystyrene requires hot wire-cutting techniques, and is used to give structure to airframe components because of its lighter weight.

wing tip side profile. These are aligned with the centerlines and fastened to the respective ends of the core, usually with nails. The hot wire rides over the edge of the templates and cuts the curvature of the wing.

There is a slight weight penalty with a foam core wing if you don't lighten the core by carving out some of the internal foam, but the ease and accuracy of construction, especially where delta and swept wings are concerned, far outweighs what is a minor disadvantage. These wing types are characteristic of many jet aircraft and the spar structure in wooden wings is much more complex than in a straight or tapered wing.

As an important safety note, it must be pointed out that hot wire cutting of foam must be reserved to polystyrene foams. Using this technique on any kind of urethane foam produces toxic gases. Polystyrene melt cutting produces gases, too, so it is a good idea to have adequate ventilation.

Carbon fiber

Carbon fiber is similar to fiberglass. It is a thin fiber that can be incorporated in a variety of forms. The basic materials are synthetics such as processed rayon which have an exceptional tensile strength requiring a great force to pull apart a cross-section. Yet carbon fiber is almost five times lighter than a comparable section of steel.

Its primary and best utilization so far is applications where bending is a factor, again because of its tensile strength. Carbon fiber was first introduced to the hobby in two forms, "tows" and thin strip sheets, 0.007 inch thick in a resin-filament matrix. The tows, or loose yarns of bundled filaments, were used in sailplane wing spars because they were subject to severe bending loads due to their wide wingspans. The tows would be sandwiched between two lightweight balsa or spruce spars with epoxy resin, and provide tremendous resistance to the flexing induced by the loads on the sailplane wing. The chief drawback to the tows was the requirement that resin be thoroughly wet to obtain the desired strength.

The strips, on the other hand, were a thin layer of parallel filaments, sometimes held together with cross strands. They were used as foam wing core spars on the surface of the cores under the balsa wing sheeting, providing almost unbreakable wings.

Today, carbon fiber is available in other forms, such as mats, blades, plates, angles and rods which make use of other advantages. In all forms except mats, carbon fiber has no memory; if it is bent, it will return to its exact shape. A good example is the use of a $5/32$ inch carbon fiber rod in place of a $5/32$ inch steel music wire landing gear leg. The carbon fiber is stronger, considerably lighter, and if subjected to horrendous bounces on takeoff or landing, will go back to its original shape—something essential for retractable landing gear so it will always return to the wheelwells when retracted. Yet, because carbon fiber will break before it can be bent to a shape, the rod is limited to applications where only a straight rod can be used.

There are disadvantages. First of all, carbon fiber is expensive, but because of its strength and light weight, a little goes a long way. Second, it is a good electrical conductor. Any of the carbon fiber powder from filing, cutting, or sanding operations should be kept away from any electronics to avoid potential shorts. In the strip form, carbon fiber splinters often occur along the edges. These are not hazardous as some rumors have it. They are like metal splinters, usually short, fine and difficult to remove. There's more hazard in a wood splinter.

When working with carbon fiber, treat it like a metal. Use hack saw blades with fine teeth to cut it, or a metal file to abrade the surface. Though it is stronger than metal, it is not as hard as metal so some care must be taken, especially when using tows around sharp corners of hard materials. All epoxies and cyanoacrylates can be used with carbon fiber successfully.

Kevlar

Kevlar's most dramatic use is with bulletproof vests that are stronger yet lighter than metal vests. It's a synthetic aramid fiber akin to nylon and comes in cloth like fiberglass. It's almost a direct replacement of glass cloth and for a weight equal to fiberglass is a little stronger but much stiffer. Kevlar could be used to build stronger, lighter fuselages, but it is preferably used with epoxy laminating resins which are more expensive than polyester. ter. Kevlar itself is also more costly than fiberglass. Consequently, it has found its prime use as an excellent stiffening reinforcement inside high stress areas of fiberglass fuselages.

Kevlar has also been used as a wing covering in lieu of fiberglass but there are two facts to consider when it's used. First, it is difficult to cut in its

This foam core shows cutouts for retract gear and a pattern of lightening *holes to decrease the weight of the wing.*

cloth form and requires special cutting shears to work it. Second, if used as a surface covering with resin, sanding it will create a fuzz that gets worse the more it's sanded. A layer of ultralight glass cloth should go over the Kevlar skin to produce a good finish.

Pressure-impregnated materials

Modelers' use of these new synthetic composite materials is unsophisticated. For example, the resin content of a given fiberglass fuselage varies from layup to layup. The ideal ratio of resin to fiberglass for premium strength at the lightest weight is rarely if ever approached due to the crude methods of cutting the cloth and applying the resin. The same is true of carbon fiber laminates or Kevlar laminates. In an airframe, adding unnecessary weight requires more strength which requires more material which requires. . . .

The aerospace industry is using similar new materials but their fabrication is more sophisticated. The same material-resin combinations are autoclaved or vacuum bagged. The autoclave is a pressurized, high-temperature process forming the best possible cure with minimum excess to yield a structure which adheres to close tolerances. A vacuum bag is a pressure device which gives the best possible adhesion between the two dissimilar materials of a composite.

These materials are generally referred to as pressure impregnated and some of them are available in finished form for our use in specialized applications. There are only a few available so they'll be briefly mentioned. Bob Violett Models produces two of these pressure-impregnated laminate materials under the Magnalite line. The first item is a fiberglass-balsa endgrain laminate. Balsa squares of equal thickness with their endgrain facing up are sandwiched between two layers of glass cloth and resin. Available in two thicknesses, 1/8 and 1/4 inch sheets, they are a replacement for plywood where equal or greater strength with less weight is needed. Since there is no grain, this material offers strength in any direction.

The other Magnalite pressure-impregnated material is a carbon fiber and engrain balsa laminate. This uses a carbon fiber mat with bidirectional fibers which sandwich endgrain balsa in an epoxy resin base. This laminate comes in only 1/4 inch thick sheets intended for high stress areas like a firewall.

Aero Composite Products sells many forms of composite materials and one form of pressure-impregnated material called Aero-panel which comes in 1/8 or 1/4 inch thick sheets. Again, thin epoxy-glass (0.010 inch thick) sheets sandwich a core, this time a high-density structural foam. Aero-panel can be used for high-strength bulkheads.

Balsa

Despite the emphasis on all the new material technology, balsa wood retains an important place in ducted-fan technology. Balsa has a strength-to-weight ratio that's still ample. It also has good vibration-dampening capability, and for the less complex designs, balsa is easier to work than creating a plug or mold and laying-up a fuselage. Coupled with several of the new composites, balsa has found even more use.

When using these materials, also use common sense to decide what's needed, whether a part needs a material with good stiffness or flexibility, strength or light weight. With all the materials available and the proper knowledge to use them, it can be fun to do some fine-tuned amateur engineering.

Adhesives

Since ducted fans have come of age, an adhesive revolution has kept apace. The epoxy and polyester resins can be used in limited ways as adhesives, but they have specialized chemical qualities which lend them to laminating large surface areas of fiberglass, Kevlar and carbon fiber.

There are other resins and adhesives better-suited to gluing joints and pieces together. Gone are the days when one type of glue had to do for everything in a model. Adhesives now work as a system with a specific type and formulation for specific applications. There are also accessories to extend the usefulness of these same adhesives.

Since the use of fiberglass is so widespread in ducted-fan modeling, let's turn to using adhesives with that. Just as the outer surface must be prepared and cleaned of any mold release, the same is true of the interior surface area where any glue joint will go. You're not dealing with mold release

The underside of the now balsa-sheeted wing reveals the landing gear *well plus the square bay for the aileron servo.*

but in some cases a waxy substance which may build up on the surface during cure of the part in the mold. If this is not removed, prior to gluing, it can affect the strength of the joint. Make it a practice to always liberally swab the glue joint area of the fiberglass piece with some sort of solvent. Alcohol, denatured alcohol, or simple white vinegar will work well. Be sure the joint is dry of any solvent before gluing begins.

Cyanoacrylate

The choice of adhesive is based on strength needs of a particular joint. Using a water-thin cyanoacrylate to glue in an engine bulkhead is asking for trouble. This type of cyano requires an absolutely tight joint where the maximum surface area of each side is in contact with one another. Inside a fiberglass fuselage, the surface is uneven, a series of high ridges and low valleys, characteristic of the weave of the fiberglass cloth. With a water-thin cyano, the joint is only on the bulkhead edge and where it meets the high ridges of the cloth weave. Using even the thicker, slower-setting cyanos risks the same type of joint. Cyanos, while they are strong, are still brittle and have less body to withstand vibration. They are excellent for tack gluing to hold something in place while another adhesive is used. It can also be handy for checking fit of parts.

Cyanoacrylates come in three viscosities, or thicknesses. The water-thin has the consistency of water, the medium cure is like syrup, and the slow cure is like a gel. Each needs to be used sparingly. Flooding a joint with

The complex shapes of jets require involved balsa frameworks, like this Folland Gnat from a Klaus Krick kit. Though balsa wood is an excellent modeling material, it is a laborious material when it comes to complex shapes.

cyano does not improve it and slows curing time. Accelerators can be used to speed a cyano cure but they also need to be used sparingly. Flooding a joint with accelerator after the application of cyano makes the cure speed up so excessively that it forms white bubble deposits which actually weaken the joint. Cyanos should also not be used on foam. Although there are specific foam primers which put a protective chemical barrier on the foam surface so the cyano doesn't attack it, the practical uses for it are minimal.

Epoxy

Epoxies come in a variety of formulations and are two parts. They're usually mixed as one or two parts resin to one part hardener. The choice depends on use. In the initial building process, most modelers use the slower-setting structural epoxies with fifteen- to thirty-minute cure times for the joints with stress or joints subject to high vibration. The slower cure allows the epoxy to settle in and effect a penetrating, complete bond. The faster, five-minute epoxies don't have the same penetrating action and are used for spot repairs. Both of these are considered structural epoxies, with the proper amount of strength and filling agents to fill in the minor imperfections in a joint better than cyanos.

Laminating epoxies, however, used in conjunction with strips of two-ounce fiberglass cloth can also provide rigid joints. Any structural epoxy is too thick to wick into the cloth. If thinned with alcohol, it risks an improper, rubbery cure which can't hold the glass cloth to the fiberglass or wood. Trying to brush in a coat of structural epoxy also pulls the weave of the cloth apart and lifts the cloth from the surface it's supposed to adhere to. The laminating epoxy, with a consistency of thin syrup, mates the glass cloth to the surfaces without tearing the weave or lifting the cloth, letting the cloth provide the strength. A joint like this could be used with some of the thicker cyanos by first providing a tack joint, then a second, filler joint, before the cloth and the laminating resin.

The rule of thumb with epoxies states that the slower the cure time, the stronger the bond. Epoxies also have sufficient body to fill in uneven gaps and create a good glue joint. Although they are brittle by themselves, they have more flexibility than the cyanos.

Silicone

One of the overlooked but reliable adhesives for strong joints is silicone, the same material used as a sealer and caulk in other applications. It has good grip and its rubbery consistency provides a natural vibration absorber. There are several drawbacks to it, however. First, it takes time to cure. Second, as it cures, it releases the fumes of its acid base. While similar to vinegar fumes, it still can corrode the plating of electrical contacts if it is near them. The best type is clear silicone sealer. Some varieties have colors in them which detract from the adhesive properties. Others are for specific applications, such as high-temperature gaskets, and are needlessly expensive.

Adhesive systems

Hobbypoxy makes three structural epoxies: Quick-Fix, Formula I and Formula II. One of its two-part epoxy paints, the clear, can be used as a quasi-laminating resin *only* when applying ultralight, 0.6 or 0.75 ounce glass cloth to sheeted structures.

Hot Stuff was the first company to introduce cyanoacrylates to the hobby. At first it produced only the water-thin type and now produces the common three viscosities. The company also provides rental tapes which demonstrate some novel, effective and practical applications of cyanoacrylates.

The ZAP line of adhesives is exclusively cyanoacrylate and was the first to introduce an extensive adhesive system with a cyano product for specific needs. Besides the three basic viscosities and accelerator, ZAP also produces a foam primer, a cyanoacrylate specifically for plastics and a special slow-cure cyano, called Flex Zap, designed primarily for work with fiberglass. When cured, it has some of the body and resilience of epoxy, and can handle vibration and stress better than other cyanos. Its strength, like any adhesive, relies on the slower cure. If accelerator is used with Flex Zap, it weakens it.

Carol Goldberg Models offers some cyanoacrylate in the basic three viscosities. While most accelerators are packaged in pump bottles to spray a fine mist, the Goldberg accelerator comes in an aerosol can.

Sig Manufacturing offers a five-minute epoxy plus the two-part Epoxolite. This two-part epoxy is a thick putty which is mixed in equal volumes. It can be buttered on where needed and is used for filling or creating small complex compounds like fairings. Surface smoothing is accomplished with small dabs of water.

Penn International Chemical (PIC), a new company in the hobby market, has introduced a total adhesive system product line of both cyanos and epoxies which also includes some accessory products. Besides epoxies with the three characteristic cure times and three cyanos in the three general viscosities, PIC also offers an epoxy laminating resin with a pot life of nine minutes which is used for quick layup jobs. There is also a hand cream which is a barrier against epoxies and cyanoacrylates.

PIC also produces Slicker, a tooling agent cream applied to specific areas needing protection against inadvertent gluing, such as the steel pins on hinges, or in pulling blind nuts tight with a screw and then gluing them. Resin Whacker is a cleaning fluid to remove unwanted epoxy or cyanoacrylate smears after the adhesive has cured.

The Loctite Corporation is another company which has recently entered the hobby market. Along with the usual three epoxies and some accessory items, Loctite makes two silicone adhesives. One is designed specifically for gluing and sealing while the other is for making gasket seals on any hot surface, such as engine manifolds or tuned pipe couplers.

Accessories

There are other products that help the glues do a better job, too. Milled fiberglass is one. It is made of ultrafine strands of chopped fiberglass and can be used with epoxy or polyester resins as a high-strength filler. A large gap in a stressed joint would need more than a glob of epoxy or a paste mixture of microballoons and resin to reinforce it. The random pattern of the tiny strands mixed with the resin in milled fiberglass form an interlocking structure that could be stronger than the material it's bonding.

Safety note

All of the new glues have more side effects than the older glues, and cyanoacrylates and epoxies can cause allergic reactions.

Cyanoacrylates give off irritating fumes when they kick off which can water eyes and sting nasal passages. They also bond skin to skin or to other surfaces. Some people use vapor mask respirators when using them; never use a dust mask, since it can actually concentrate the fumes instead of blocking them.

Epoxies are known for their potential to cause allergic reactions, and the the formulations for each kind are different enough to present more potential for a problem to occur than with cyanos. Sometimes, the reaction is immediate and severe when first used. Other times, it is a cumulative process which can suddenly erupt into a serious reaction. My purpose here is not to alarm, merely to advise you to take sensible precautions.

Chapter 6

Equipment installation and fine-tuning

Setting-up a ducted-fan plane does not take special ingenuity or skills but it does take thoughtful preparation and learning to work from the inside-out. Part of this chapter will deal with extra considerations peculiar to ducted-fan aircraft and offer some practical methods learned from the experience of other modelers.

There is one important consideration before the kit box or any work begins—safety. While all the materials and accessories mentioned are safe to use, they do require proper handling, and all through this chapter reference will be made to the safe handling or operation of ducted-fan models. Manufacturers have gone to great lengths to provide instructions for the proper use of them but it's the modeler's responsibility to use these products in a sensible and thoughtful way. For example, the higher than normal speeds which these models operate at are not unsafe. It is the inability or inexperience of the modeler operating them improperly which could make them dangerous. Common sense is imperative.

Ductwork

The complexity of building ducted-fan models is not in the construction, it's in the equipment installation. Most of the techniques used in building a

Side inlets are probably the most common form for bringing the air into the fuselage as shown on this Jet Model Products Starfire. The actual shape doesn't matter as long as it provides sufficient air.

propeller model can be used in building a fan model. The unique part of the construction, unlike other planes, is the thrust tube and, if the plane needs it, a full inlet. Depending on the kit, these items are made from either Lexan, 1/64 inch thick plywood or a single layer of two- or four-ounce glass cloth laid-up over a male plug of the part. Each manufacturer has its own method of installing ductwork but there are similarities.

The thrust tube is used on all fans and is a permanent installation. Of course, provision is always made to gain access to the engine and also to remove the fan for maintenance. The first requirement for any thrust tubes used with tractor fans is that they be fuel-proofed. With a fiberglass or Lexan tube, that's already done. With a plywood tube, it's necessary to pre-paint the inside of the tube before it's assembled. Otherwise, the fuel-oil mix blown out of the tuned pipe will saturate the inside tube adding to weight and also to a tail-heavy aircraft.

To make a plywood tube, simply cut the pattern provided in the model's plans. Once the pattern is cut, a 1/64 thick plywood strip of 1 to 1 1/2 inches in width is glued along one edge so that it forms a flange on the outside edge of the tube. Rolling the tube is aided by a simple jig to hold the tube in shape while the seam line is sealed. The two edges should fit closely but a perfect fit is not necessary since the flange seals the seam.

If the model is a Byron Originals kit, the thrust tube is made of Lexan sheet plastic. This material works well but the seam has a tendency to split or blow out. The overlapped edges of the plastic sheet form the seam which is glued on the inside and reinforced on the outside with a thin strip of tape. For extra insurance, a length of two-inch-wide package sealing tape applied to the outside and inside seam will extend the life of the thrust tube.

This is the single fiberglass internal duct for the Starfire. Note the transition from the rectangular shapes to the single circular tube.

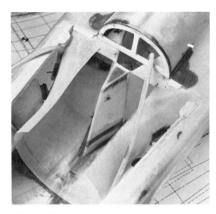

Ideally, the air from side inlets should be kept separated right up to the face of the fan impeller. That's where a splitter plate comes in, like that held here. It must be removable, however, so there is access to the spinner for starting the engine.

The splitter plate is in place in the duct. It keeps the air separated up to the spinner and helps lessen the turbulent flow that can be caused by the mixture of the two air streams.

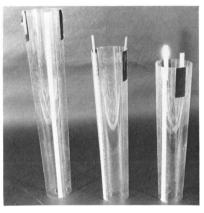

This shows the wooden thrust tube and engine hatch of the earlier Jet Model Products Starfire. The tube is 1/64 inch plywood rolled and glued together along a center seam. A strip of ply along the length of the seam serves as a flange. The frame around the front of the tube is a fan access hatch which is cut out. There's a mirror image frame that remains on the thrust tube. The fiberglass engine cover cap on top of the thrust tube later is cut out also. The thrust tube is cut in half, front and back, and the rear half first glued into the tailpipe of the airframe. A flange is glued around the rear of the front section and then slipped into the fuselage and over the rear tube section.

The Byron thrust tubes are made from rolled Lexan and are sized to the length of the fuselage. They slip over the rear of the Byro-Jet shroud and the two metal "ears" are screwed to the bulkhead mount. The seam in the tube must be reinforced with package tape since the pressure of the exhaust air can blow the tube apart, killing thrust.

For tractor fans with the thrust tube overlapping the rear of the fan shroud, an engine hatch access must be cut out. The size of the hatch must be large enough so that the fan unit can be lifted out of the model. A large hatch will also provide access to the cylinder head, carburetor (as long as it's a rear-carb engine) and tuned pipe coupling.

To construct the hatch in a plywood tube, a double framework is glued around the outline of the hatch area. This framework will stiffen and maintain the shape of the piece of the tube which is cut out and will also stiffen the section of the remaining tube where the hatch will mate. It is important not to glue the two frameworks together. A small clearance between the frame of the hatch and the frame of the main thrust tube allows an X-ACTO saw to fit between them to cut out the hatch.

With a fiberglass thrust tube, the hatch area maintains its shape because it is made of molded fiberglass. Using a pattern, simply cut out the hatch from the rolled fiberglass tube. To provide some rigidity, a strip of fiberglass or thin 1/64 plywood is glued around the perimeter of the hatch to act as a flange and overlap the main thrust tube.

Either type of hatch, fiberglass or plywood, usually has a molded-fiberglass cylinder head fairing positioned and glued over a cutout in the hatch for the cylinder head. Besides providing clearance, the fairing also channels the air over the cylinder head. Centered directly over the glow plug in the cylinder head is a small circular cutout for a glow plug wrench. The diameter should be as small as possible to minimize air leakage. Most manufacturers of tractor fans provide these molded-fiberglass cylinder head fairings for their particular fan unit, so any scratchbuilt ducted-fan model can benefit from one without having to make one.

The earlier fan impellers, especially the Axiflo 20, required some sizing to obtain the proper diameter. Equal blade length was critical; use of a drill press and sanding block ensure this. Diameter is decreased in very gradual increments.

Getting the thrust tube inside the aircraft is not as difficult as it may seem. Almost all tubes, except for the Byron Originals Lexan tubes, are installed in two pieces. Fiberglass tubes are made in two sections and there is usually a female flange on the end of one, which overlaps the edge of the other section.

If it's a plywood tube, the single piece is cut in two somewhere along its length. A thin strip of $1/64$ plywood, about $3/4$ inch wide and equal in length to the circumference of the tube, is wrapped around the end of one of the two sections to act as a flange, just as on the fiberglass tube.

In both cases, the rear of the tube is installed first, then the front section with the engine access hatch is slipped into the rear using epoxy to adhere the joint. It's best not to use cyanoacrylate for this joint since you need time to work the two sections into alignment. Before the thrust tube is glued or fastened to the airframe, it's slipped over the mounted fan unit and positioned.

Once the tube is in place and aligned, it can be tied to the tailpipe bulkhead and the rear fan bulkhead with strips of two-ounce fiberglass cloth, laid in place and glued with epoxy or cyanoacrylate. There's usually some clearance in the holes of these bulkheads so the thrust tube is not too tight a fit. Once held in place with the fiberglass strips, the clearance can then be filled with Epoxolite or polyester body filler. If the shape of the tube is distorted when doing this, thrust will be lost through the drag of turbulent flow.

Fan setup and balancing

At the rpm which ducted fans turn, it's essential that their impellers be as balanced as possible and that the proper tip clearance from the shroud be maintained. The newer fan units, like the Viojett and the Dynamax, have impellers which have already been balanced and assembled. Any of the others, however, do need to be checked and balanced.

The impeller and the spinner are a unit and should be assembled when the balance is done. There are two ways of providing the needed weight adjustment and both have their pros and cons. One method is to find the heavy blade and drill lightening holes in the vertical web of the hub opposite the heavy blade until balanced. The danger is that the hub can be weakened in the area of a blade root and the blade could fail. If this method is chosen, care must be taken that any lightening holes be drilled so they don't pass directly under a blade and don't get too close to the hub. Don't use a drill bit any thicker than $1/4$ inch.

The other method of balancing an impeller is to add weight instead of subtracting it. Lead shot or small bits of plumber's solder are added to counterbalance the heavy side. The danger with this method is that the shot or solder can come loose with vibration. For insurance, do not use five-minute epoxy or cyanoacrylate. Clean the area where the weight will be glued with solvent such as alcohol or acetone. Then rough up the surface with sandpaper before gluing. Allowance must be made for the weight of the epoxy. Some people dimple the glue area with a drill bit to form a shallow pocket for the weight and the glue.

Trying to balance by adding or subtracting weight directly opposite the light or heavy blade usually involves a vicious cycle. As one balance is achieved with two blades, another blade may become heavy, and so on. The solution to the problem is, for lack of a better term, the 120 degree method. It simply means the position of the added weight or subtracted weight is split evenly and placed at angles of 120 degrees on the hub. It's the same method used when balancing an automobile tire.

If weight is to be subtracted from the heavy blade side, an equal number of lightening holes are drilled and equally spaced on either side of the heavy blade and separated by an angle of 120 degrees from the center of the impeller. If weight is added, it's added equally to either side of the heavy blade at an angle of 120 degrees.

Tip clearance between the blades and the shroud is important. Fan manufacturers give the tolerances for the clearance. For the Viojett unit, the clearance is preset and no adjustment need be made. For those that need it, the clearance should be done before the impeller is balanced. There are also two methods for doing this.

Earlier impeller casting was not precise enough to ensure a balanced impeller. This Byron unit is being checked for balance in a High Point balancer, the only kind capable of precise balancing. Note the white mark on the hub, painted with typists correction fluid, which denotes the heavy blade.

The first requires that the impeller be chucked into a drill press to provide a wobble-free rotation. Most impeller shaft holes have a diameter of $1/4$ inch, so a simple $1/4$ inch bolt can be used as the shaft needed to support the impeller in the drill chuck. A block of hardwood, faced on one side with 80 grit sandpaper, is laid on the drill press table. With the impeller chucked and rotating in the drill press, the sanding block is carefully moved tangent to the spinning edges of the impeller blades. Only a fraction of the blade tips should be removed at any time, and the clearance constantly checked in the fan shroud. Automotive feeler gauges, like those used for spark plugs, work well.

The other method of providing proper clearance for the blade tip requires that the impeller, without the spinner, be mounted inside the shroud. A single piece of 400 grit Wetodry sandpaper is slipped between the inner surface of the shroud and the blade tips. The impeller is then turned while the sandpaper is held in place. A socket wrench which fits the impeller retaining nut may be needed to turn the impeller until it rotates freely.

A $1/4$ inch hole has been drilled in the web of the impeller hub on this Byron impeller. It's on the heavy blade, denoted by the white mark. The balancing is a gradual refining process going from one blade to another, and another. The latest fans, the Dynamax, the Viojett and the Hurricane, do not require balancing.

This photograph shows the fuel tank and manifold installation in a Byron model. The fuel tank sits forward on the top of the fuselage while the fuel filler manifold is at the upper right corner. The Byron tank is actually two tanks in one, and holds 24 ounces.

This photograph shows the formed fiberglass engine hatch cover on a Viojett. This hatch also gives access to the tuned pipe for easier positioning. The hatch is held in place with O-rings fastened around specially molded brackets.

In both cases, it's essential to remove only a little material at a time and to do it evenly. It may be tedious but the alternative is to remove too much and ruin the impeller.

In no case should material be shaved from any part of the blade, or the blade sanded along its surface area. This creates an imbalance among the individual blades which would be difficult to correct. It also ruins the aerodynamic shape of the blade. About the only material that should ever be shaved is flashing, a remote possibility on the precision-cast impellers.

The final consideration in the fan setup is the mounting of the tuned pipe. The most recent trend in fan units is to provide a pipe that is pre-adjusted to the specific engine and does not require any experimentation with pipe length. The Viojett/KBV .72 combination is a good example. The header pipe on the engine manifold has two O-ring positions, rearward for regular operation and forward for hot, humid conditions.

When installing any pipe with an O-ring seal on the header pipe, use the lubricant called for in the manufacturer's instructions. If the O-ring is damaged in any way, it will affect the operation of the tuned pipe. It's a good idea to have a supply of these O-rings and check them often.

The rear of the tuned pipe, in a tractor fan, is usually fastened at the stinger or actual exhaust outlet. A bracket is fastened to a position in the thrust tube directly over the stinger. This bracket's shape allows an O-ring

Tuned pipes must be supported somehow in the aircraft and there are different mounting methods. This photo shows the Byron pipe mount for the Byro-Jet. It is a formed sheet metal standoff that gets screwed to a mounting surface in the fuselage.

Shown here is a popular style of mounting bracket for pipes inside the thrust tube on tractor fans. The plate is plywood with the circular notch cut. A foot (end view) serves as non-slipping base for the pipe stringer, and a simple O-ring holds the pipe in place.

to be hooked over the stinger and a cutout in the bracket. The tension of the rubber O-ring holds the stinger to the end of the bracket.

With the Byron pusher fan and its specially shaped pipe, a standoff, or support, is glued in a position near the end of the pipe and the pipe fastened to it, usually with a bracket. The Byron pipe uses a telescoping coupler which makes adjustment easier. It is important with the Byron pipe setup

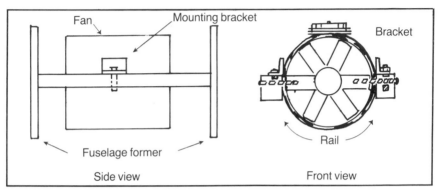

Rail-mounting method for fans. This method is used only with tractor fans.

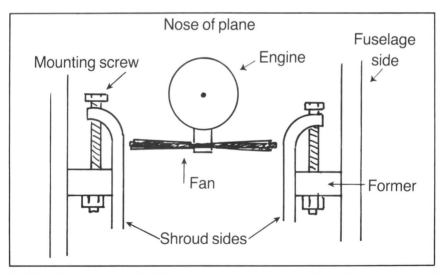

Bulkhead-mounting method for fans. This method is used primarily for *pusher fans although it may be used for either assembly.*

that the pipe receive enough cooling air. In some Byron installations, there are no intake arrangements with airflow to pass adequately over the pipe. The result is an extremely hot pipe which can shift because the silicone tuned pipe coupler softens and expands. When this happens, it cannot hold the precise adjustment of the pipe length. Opening a small hole forward of the pipe and backing it with a baffle to direct the airflow over it will provide plenty of cooling air.

Radios

A wide range of radio equipment, from the most complex to the simple four-channel radio, can be used with ducted fans. The only real requirement is absolute dependability, a logical concern because of the investment. The super radios are not required except with the most complex aircraft such as Jack Tse's swing-wing F-14 which requires a preprogrammed module to monitor and adjust the mixing rates of some of the control surfaces.

While a simple four-channel can fly most jets without retracts, for those who intend to do more than a jet or two, it would be convenient to use some of the latest radios with simple mixing, servo reversing and dual rates. A six-channel is good with the extra two channels for retracts or flaps, but a seven-channel usually offers the best all-around convenience package with almost every desired feature.

One of the most exotic radios is the Futaba eight-channel PCM. It has all the special features—and more—that a fan modeler could use. A radio like this is not essential to fly fans. The only criteria is good reliability.

Servo selection must be more precise in fans because of the high vibration, the tight confined spaces and the greater than usual airloads placed on flying surfaces. These Futaba servos represent the gamut from the huge S-34 quarter-scale servo on the left, to the standard S-28 in the center and the powerful but smaller S-30 on the right.

129

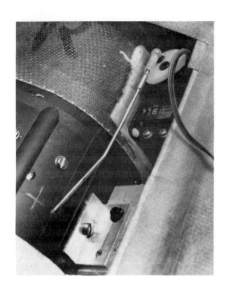

Servos get put wherever they fit. One way to get an easy throttle pushrod run to the throttle arm is to mount the servo right on the intake liner of the thrust tube.

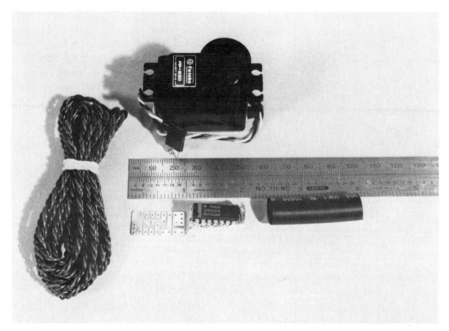

The long servo leads found many times in fan aircraft can cause radio interference, so the use of noise suppressors like the ACE Noise Trap (shown in kit form here) is prudent. The device is inserted inline on the servo cable.

It would be wise to investigate the current frequency regulations before buying or setting up a system. Much has been written in the model magazines about the changes which take place in 1988. Some of the lower 72 MHz channels, Channels 12 to 34, will be narrow band (only 20 kHz frequency spacing) while Channels 38 to 56 will continue to operate in the current spacing until 1991 when they too become narrow band. Incorrect frequencies could ruin an otherwise flawless setup.

While choice of a transmitter-receiver combination is wide, the choice of servos is more specific and critical, especially in their use for higher load applications. The loads imposed on ducted-fan control surfaces are generally greater than with most other modeling applications. Model speed and, in the case of stabilators, their surface area, need strong vibration-tolerant servos. The servo's force is measured in ounce-inches of torque, and weak servos cannot deal with the necessity of resisting flutter. In the case of ailerons and conventional elevators of medium-size jets, servos of at least forty to forty-five ounce-inches of torque should be adequate. On larger stabilators, a fifty to fifty-five ounce-inch servo is insurance against flutter and a stalled servo due to excessive loads. When the aircraft become large, such as Byron Originals' F-15 or Jet Model Products' F-4 Phantom, which both use stabilator surfaces, a single, large, quarter-scale servo of 100 to 115 ounce-inches is sufficient. Two fifty to fifty-five ounce-inch servos could also be harnessed in tandem with a Y connector.

When it comes to aileron servos, the popularity of plug-in wings for ducted fans has led to the use of an aileron servo in each wing panel driving its respective aileron. A forty to forty-five ounce-inch servo is sufficient. Most of the Byron Originals jets, however, use a single aileron servo to drive their plug-in aileron connections. If used in the standard configuration, the aileron servo should be at least fifty to fifty-five ounce-inches.

In any of the other applications, rudder, nose wheel steering, retract valve operation, throttle and so on, standard servos are sufficient since there is no critical or excessive load placed on them. Still, all of the servos should be vibration tolerant. There seem to be more potential vibration problems with the coreless motor servos in fiberglass fuselages as they are affected by the high-frequency vibration. A standard servo motor seems to tolerate the vibration better. Besides this consideration, ball-bearing-supported output shafts on the servo are desirable but not a requirement.

Coupled to the servo choice is the use of an adequate pushrod system beginning with the gears on the servos. If possible, use servos with metal gears for anything which experiences a heavy load like aileron, stabilator or elevator. Metal gears resist shearing better than nylon gears.

Servo output arms are also vital. A wheel output is more rigid than an arm output. It has more mass to resist bending or torquing and can support the weight of the pushrod.

On any control surface, the stronger, more rigid pushrod is better. A rigid pushrod does not allow any bowing or bending when the control surface is under load. Aluminum or fiberglass arrow shafts and, more recently,

131

hollow carbon fiber shafts are the best choices. Unfortunately, they require a direct line from servo to control horn, something that is not often possible in ducted fans unless there is room to spot servos around the fuselage in places where they have a direct run to the attachment point on the control surface.

Plastic pushrods for control surfaces are the last resort. Although they can be made rigid enough by firmly anchoring the outer sheath in several places along its length, they expand and contract with temperature changes, and alter the trim setting of the model. With a high-performance plane, like many of the fan aircraft, being out of trim can lead to a quick crash. Music wire of 1/16 inch diameter is more acceptable but must be supported either in a sheath or by standoffs along its length to prevent bowing.

Unlike propeller models, there are no traditional places to locate radio equipment in fan models. Sometimes the particular model may allow the placement of receiver, servos and battery all in one radio compartment. Because this equipment gets moved around to wherever there is a practical fit, it requires intelligent consideration of several factors, which interact with one another.

The center of gravity must always be considered when placing servos. For example, placing two large servos in the extreme tail for conveniently controlling the elevator and the rudder, would probably make the model tail-heavy. To compensate, the battery pack would then have to be placed as far forward in the nose as possible, probably with additional weight to balance the model. This would add needless extra weight and possibly lose some of the battery current due to the longer electrical cable's resistance. Although it would be more difficult to access, it might be better to place the servos behind the fan unit, between the exhaust tube and the fuselage skin.

Besides CG, servo cable lengths and antenna runs are a subtle yet potentially dangerous factor to consider. Any servo cable over twelve inches runs the risk of acting as a secondary antenna, so it must be grounded or

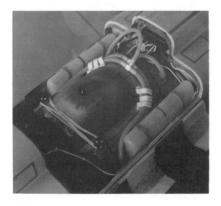

Neatness counts in a fan and helps eliminate some of the maintenance bugs. It only takes a little forethought instead of simply jamming everything in. Cardinal rule is to keep everything fastened down; don't let anything dangle.

isolated from the true antenna. One way of doing this is to substitute a shielded servo cable, adding a fourth, sometimes braided flexible, wire over the three wires for the servo. The fourth wire attaches to the negative servo wire at the receiver end and runs the entire length of the servo cable and is left unattached.

In a fan model, the antenna is usually run inside the fuselage. Due to better signal selectivity, this overcomes reception problems, except in conjunction with long servo leads. As long as the servo lead is shielded or separated from the servo cables and not run parallel to them, there is no loss in antenna receptivity.

One important concern, however, is making certain the antenna is stretched out in a straight line and has no chance of coming loose to be sucked into the fan. The most common installation is to run the antenna inside a plastic sheath securely glued to the inner skin of the fuselage.

Batteries can still be the weakest link in the entire radio system and again, because of the higher than normal expense in many ducted fans, it pays in the long run to buy quality batteries, and plenty of capacity is a prime requirement. Even if the plane is a simple four-servo model, the loads which the servos are subject to place more than the usual electrical demand

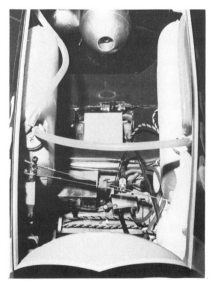

This Jet Hangar F-86 shows a tight installation because retracts have also been added. Note servo placement and saddle tank installation for the Turbax I fan.

From this one location in a Jet Model F-4 Phantom, five servos control the throttle, the drag chute, the elevator and the retracts. Note that each has been sized according to its job with the elevator servo being a massive Futaba S-34.

on them. With some of the complex models, with anywhere from six to twelve servos, that electrical demand skyrockets. A 500 milliamp hours (mAh) battery pack is the minimum for a four-servo model. Anything beyond that should have a larger capacity battery or redundant battery systems. For a six-servo plane with retracts, flap, extra aileron servos or all three, at least a 900 mAh battery should be used. Any greater number of servos would work best with a 1200 mAh pack or a redundant battery system.

With any of the electronic components, installation must take into account the unique factors of a ducted-fan model. High-frequency vibration in a fan requires that the receiver and the battery be substantially wrapped in foam. The foam should not be compressed or it is robbed of vibration-dampening qualities. A good target figure for the foam is about a 1/2 inch thickness all the way around.

Servo trays are sometimes mounted to the fuselage inner skin, and they must be firmly attached. Bedding the tray in a little silicone or epoxy works well. If you use silicone, remember that the fumes it gives off during its cure are corrosive to electrical components, especially in a confined area. As an added reinforcement of the servo tray, lay a strip of two-ounce glass cloth over the plate of the servo tray. Also, keep the servo wire cables firmly attached to something solid, especially in installations with no intake ducting. Don't leave any possibility of wires flailing around inside the fuselage. Simple strapping tape with a strong adhesion or balsa standoffs can be used to adhere the wires in several places along the length of their run.

Not only is rigidity necessary in the pushrod for control surfaces, it is also required on the servo output arm. The straight outputs on the left and right are less favored than the much stronger wheel output in the center which cannot torque and twist under loads as can the others.

Internal parts

Some of the kits available offer a fiberglass fuselage without the internal bulkheads installed. The full-size plans of the model usually show the positioning, and many of the fuselages will have position marks scribed or molded into the fuselage itself to get exact positioning. If there are no marks, reference lines can be drawn using one of the Sharpie fine-line permanent markers and a flexible piece of plastic with a straight edge. This marker readily washes off fiberglass using denatured alcohol or acetone on a rag or piece of paper towel. Another alternative is to use thin Chart Pak tape to mark the reference lines.

Since all the fiberglass parts are semitransparent, it's easy to line up the internal parts. The fit of these parts should be comfortable, not too snug. If there's a tight fit, the part will bulge the fuselage surface and it's never that noticeable until after the finish is applied. Even if there is a slight gap, a slurry mix of epoxy and microballoons will fill the void.

For a really strong filler, Bob Violett Models sells ultrafine chopped strands of glass fiber $1/32$ inch long. When mixed in the proper volume with epoxy, it can provide a filler that creates a tremendously strong joint. When working with the Violett glass fibers, use a dust mask and always open the jar slowly and carefully! These fibers are extremely light and can blow around easily, moreso than microballoons. This makes them easy to breathe in. They are not toxic but a sufficient amount could cause respiratory irritation.

Control surface balance

Many of the jet model kits use foam as the wing structure base. Some are cut out of light, expanded-bead polystyrene foam and must be sheeted with balsa or covered with $1 1/2$ or 2 ounce per square yard fiberglass. If the fiberglass method is chosen, the resin used to fix the cloth to the foam must not attack it! It must be compatible. Paints with high thinner or reducer content will dissolve the foam.

The Byron Originals planes use a denser, more rigid injection-molded foam. These can then be covered with a low-heat, shrinkable plastic. While the shorter wingspans do have the required rigidity, the longer wingspans with only the plastic covering have a tendency to twist under the load of an aileron or at high speeds. It is safer to sheet the wing with balsa (even $1/32$ inch) or with the fiberglass cloth method. It is also extra insurance to substitute wood trailing edges near control surfaces and wood leading edges for the control surfaces themselves. At high speeds, the wood gives a better hinging surface.

Some extra effort must be spent with control surface installation. It should be repeated that the higher speeds of ducted-fan planes bring them closer to the potential for flutter. Rigid pushrods, clevises that are attached as far out on servo arms and control horns as possible, rigid servo arms and control horns that do not flex, and direct, straight runs help reduce the potential but do not eliminate it.

The best prevention is balance of the control surfaces, which is a necessity with stabilators even if the plans do not call for it. In the case of ailerons and conventional elevators, sealing the gap in the hinge line will also help. The latter often involves using a mylar heat-shrinkable plastic in a crossover pattern to seal the gap. The alternative method is to first install the aileron, and then carefully glue triangular stock to the trailing edge of the wing to form a pocket for the leading edge of the aileron. The same method can be used for a conventional elevator or rudder.

Balance of the control surface is probably the most effective means of counteracting flutter and it is necessary with the larger surface of a stabilator. Mass-balancing is the technique used and is done by adding weight to the control surface forward of the hinge line or pivot point. A simple length of $1/16$ inch music wire is glued into the leading edge of the control surface and run forward of the hinge line. A small lead weight is then soldered or glued to the tip of the music wire to provide the proper balance.

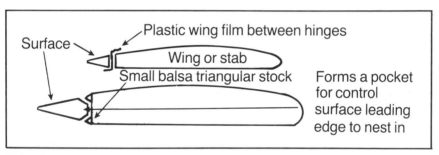

Control surface gap sealing.

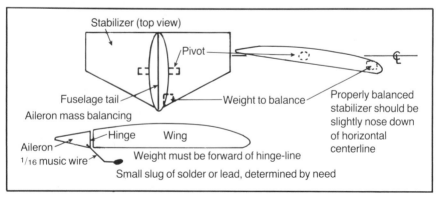

Control surface balancing methods.

With a stabilator, weight is added to a hole drilled horizontally in the root of the control surface at its leading edge. In this case, the required balance doesn't mean that the surface remains level on its pivot point. The leading edge should actually droop five degrees down to eliminate any flutter.

Retracts

Most ducted-fan planes use pneumatic retracts as an option. The mechanical retracts with their necessity for pushrod linkage are difficult to utilize. It's much easier to run flexible plastic tubing for air lines than it is to design bends into rigid music wire as pushrod linkage.

Reproducing the gear of many modern full-size jets is next to impossible without access to someone with special metal-working skills. The complex geometries of the retraction sequence into the fuselage versus the wing would be costly. Consequently, most scale modelers adapt existing gear as best they can.

The main gear in a wing is usually mounted to a plywood plate, while the nose gear is attached to a vertical former or horizontal plate. In a regular

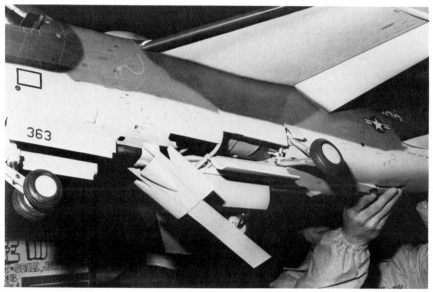

Because most real fighter jets have very thin wings, the main landing gear is usually placed in the belly of the plane. That presents problems for a ducted-fan modeler, as with this Jet Hangar

Hobbies A-7D Corsair, both in the complexity of the gear mechanism and the availability of space to simply tuck the gear.

wooden wing, the plate is supported between two ribs just aft of the CG and the main spar. In a foam wing, holes for the air lines and the outline of the plate and retract unit must be cut out of the foam core before sheeting the wing. The plate outline and retract outline are cut with a hot wire following a template layed down on the core. The long horizontal holes for the air lines can be drilled with a length of brass tubing that's been sharpened at one end, or with a hot rod to melt the hole into the foam.

Most pneumatic units have two lines to each retract unit to push the gear down, then push it back up. To save effort, the down lines are usually restricted to one color while the up lines use another. Spring Air retracts have only a single line, to push and hold the retracts up. To get the gear down, the air pressure is released and the spring action in the gear drops them.

The biggest problem in a pneumatic system is leakage at a number of spots. The O-ring seal inside the air cylinder can deteriorate and lose air; the same is true for the shunting valve. The air lines can also spring leaks, usually around the nipples on the hardware.

Preventative maintenance is the best method of ensuring reliable operation. Some modelers lubricate the internal surface of the retract actuating cylinder by spraying a pure silicone lubricant into it. This helps eliminate

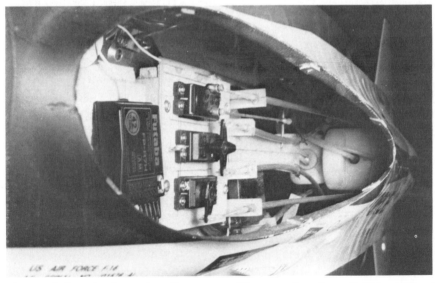

Many of the single-engine Byron planes have been standardized on placing most of the radio gear right under the floor of a removable canopy.

That requires long flexible pushrod runs, however, and the consequent necessity of firmly anchoring these in many spots.

Retracts get mounted in various ways. This photograph shows the special bracket in the Byron F-16 which mounts the Rhom air retract mechanism.

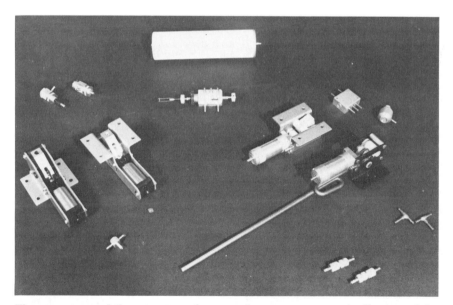

These are some of the retract mechanisms being used today. On the left are the Spring Air retracts which use only a single pneumatic line to force the gear up. In the event of pressure loss, the gears automatically extend because they're spring-loaded. The Rhom Air gear on the right uses the more conventional two-line pneumatic system.

the formation of rust on the internal surface which can chew up the rubber O-ring. This does not mean the cylinder is taken apart. A short length of air line is connected at one end to the plastic probes that usually come with aerosol solvents and lubricants and at the other end to one of the nipples of the actuating cylinder. The spray should be pure silicone, not one with any sort of penetrating oil, since the solvent action of the oil could soften, expand or dissolve the O-ring. Spring Air retracts do not require lubrication.

To prevent belly-up landings, it's best to periodically check the system to ensure that it's holding pressure. Pump it up to 100 psi and time the release of system pressure. A new system should hold the pressure indefinitely. A change of 20 psi over a ten- to fifteen-minute span means that there is a small leak beginning that could get worse. Also know how many cycles or up-and-down retraction sequences your air reservoir can support before it loses sufficient operating pressure. This can be an indicator of a beginning leak, too.

To find the leak is not always simple. Like automotive tires, you can apply a soapy solution to the lines and check for bubbles that betray leaks. Try to keep any soap residue to a minimum since the chemicals in the soaps can corrode some metals over an extended period of time. Since the air lines are transparent, a visual check for dark streaks can point to nicks or splits in the line which can cause leakage.

Probably the best preventative maintenance, however, is making sure the gear legs and wheels do not bind during retraction or extension. The wheel and strut wells should have at least a 1/4 inch clearance between the surface of the well and the wheel or gear strut itself to allow for any bending of the gear leg. In this case, more is better and the clearances should be adjusted to the type of field the plane operates from. Paved runways can use the minimal clearance because there is less of a chance of bending gear legs.

Most ducted fans require some sort of cradle. Even a crude one like this made out of scrap foam is invaluable for keeping surfaces free from scratches. It also provides easy maintenance.

On a grass runway the clearances should be increased because of the higher stress put on the gear.

To help the gear leg bending problem, there are two solutions. The first is the use of 1/4 inch carbon fiber rod to replace the gear legs themselves. The rod can bend and flex, but it has no memory so it cannot be deformed and will always return to the same position. The problem is finding a way to incorporate the ninety-degree bend for an axle.

The other solution is the flex plate method introduced by Bob Violett with his Magnalite carbon fiber flex plate. Made of carbon fiber composite, the plate is firmly attached to a spar or bulkhead in the fuselage or wing. The gear mechanism is then mounted directly to the plate. As with the carbon fiber gear leg, the plate can flex like a stiff spring but it has no memory and returns to the same position no matter what stress is put on it.

Finishing

With all the internal equipment and structure installed, it's time to finish the model. With a wood structure, there is a choice of using one of the heat-shrinkable mylar plastics or painting a finish on. The former option excludes all the fabric coverings because of their finish texture (most un-jet-like) and their added weight. The exception is Coverite's Micafilm, a strong

Shown here is the engine hatch cover on a Dynamax fan being screwed back into position. The hatch cover is usu- *ally a molded fiberglass part fitted over the forward top of the thrust tube.*

covering that can be easily painted. Using one of these mylars gives the lightest finish, and most of them can be painted on with the two-part epoxy paints for detail trim.

If the choice is paint, then the woodgrain must be filled. There are many methods, some quite old and some more recent. One method in particular has proven effective and quick. Ultralight glass cloth (0.5 to 0.6 ounce per square yard) is draped over the airframe and adhered with laminating resin. The preference is epoxy since polyester sometimes has curing problems with other adhesives and fillers used with models. The alternative is to brush on clear epoxy paint first to adhere it, and then brush over that with the laminating resin.

There's usually not much base finish preparation for a fiberglass fuselage but the pin holes must be filled. These tiny voids in the surface layer of the fuselage are usually few and far between on quality fiberglass work, but they are there and difficult to see before the model is painted. If ignored, they have a remarkable way of becoming unsightly after the last coat of paint is on.

One of the few remaining hurdles and a critical factor in popular acceptance of fans is noise. They are loud and their high frequency can be more than annoying—it can harm hearing. Good sense dictates some sort of hearing protection like that worn here by Ron Kemp, left, and Mark Frankel, right.

The usual method of finding and filling these pin holes is to first paint the fiberglass part with a sandable primer. The opaque texture of the surface shows the pin holes. Spackling compound or any other suitable filler that can be readily sanded may then be used to fill the voids. Once filled, the primer coat and filler patches are sanded down to the glass surface. Another coat of primer is applied and checked for pin holes. This second primer coat can be the actual base color coat of the plane. Any pin holes left are filled and then sanded down.

A new product designed specifically for filling pin holes is the Bob Violett Models Pin Hole Filler. Instead of laying down a primer coat, the fuselage is first cleaned with a solvent, and then lightly scuffed with 320 grit Wetodry sandpaper. The pin hole filler is then smeared over the fiberglass part with a paper towel and left to dry for an hour. The dried paste is then wiped off completely and the first primer coat applied. The dried paste *cannot* be cleaned off with a solvent or it will pull a little bit of the filler in the pin hole out with it. Finally, the first primer coat is applied. If needed, some of the pin hole filler material can then be used to dab any of the spots missed in the initial application.

Noise

Perhaps the most overlooked and potentially dangerous hazard with fans is their noise levels and frequency. International competition rules are fostering a trend toward quieter engines. Four-stroke engines, with their quiet operation, are becoming increasingly popular. The trend to quiet operation recognizes that hearing can be damaged with noisy equipment. Unfortunately, ducted fans have not been able to follow that trend yet.

While the measurement of the noise levels of ducted-fan engines is not excessive, two other factors make their noise potentially harmful. First, the sound of the air being accelerated to higher velocities than with a prop causes a greater degree of noise. Second, the higher rpm of the fan itself causes a high-pitched sound which can be more grating than lower-pitched sounds. The problem is exaggerated by the fact that the sound-producing element is situated inside the fuselage, most often a brittle fiberglass unit which acts as a resonating sounding board.

My point is to promote the use of hearing protection devices like those commonly used in other high-noise practices. These protection earphones can be purchased at gun shops, tool supply stores or hardware stores since their need is being recognized even in home use.

Safety note

With the earlier fan units using regular tuned pipes with headers that needed cutting, it was customary to construct some sort of bench running stand for the fan so that the proper pipe length and mixture adjustments could be figured out. The practice was questionable because the bench setup could never duplicate the intake arrangement of the particular aircraft. As mentioned earlier, this static condition required a bellmouth inlet to get the best airflow into the fan face, something that would again change the conditions of the fan installation in the aircraft. Some manufacturers strongly suggest that you do not bench-run their fan unit, especially the recent products which have most of the setup work designed out of them.

One other reason that bench-running is used less is the amount of suction created by fans. Equipment in a non-intake-duct arrangement and cabling must be securely fastened so that they do not flap around in the airflow or get sucked into the fan. This same precaution extends to pieces of clothing, long hair or fingers. Never work over an operating fan with anything dangling. If sucked in, it may shatter the blade or drag a finger into the spinning fan. These precautions apply mainly to aircraft with cheater holes where the fan is exposed. Yet even with a fully ducted system, something can get sucked in an intake and damage or destroy the fan.

Chapter 7

Flying

There's nothing magical about flying ducted-fan airplanes. Many of the same operating practices used with other two-cycle glow engines and aircraft can be used with fan planes. But there are several unique aspects.

At the high rpm-range of fan planes, it is difficult to get a correct needle setting using the traditional method of listening for the aural change from the four-cycle to the two-cycle. A ballpark mixture can be dialed in, but the final setting should be adjusted with an optical tachometer. There is some trial-and-error adjustment, even with the tach, until the engine runs well. The tach can then be used to repeat settings for quick and precise adjustment.

The logic circuit of most tachs, however, is designed to compute the rpm of two-bladed propellers. Since fans use five, seven or eleven blades, the readings would be wrong if they were taken from the spinning blades. Instead, a white stripe is painted on the impeller spinner or hub. The reading from this single white stripe should be multiplied by two to get the correct reading. Two stripes can be painted on, 180 degrees from each other, and the reading is then exact. The rpm-range of the tachometer selected should be able to read at least to 25,000 or 26,000 rpm.

Starting the fan is different from regular models although the engine still must be primed. With tractor engines mounted behind the fan, the engine access hatch on the fuselage is always removed. The priming technique varies from fan to fan and engine to engine; it's best to refer to the manufacturer's instructions. All fan engines should start quickly. If they don't, do not keep trying to turn the engine over. Check the glow plug, needle valve settings, fuel plumbing or pipe coupling to make sure everything is OK. Continually spinning the impeller will flood the engine.

Until 1984, the only fan unit that had a specialized starter was the Byron unit. Since it was a pusher fan with the engine ahead of the impeller, the only access to the impeller was through the tailpipe. A starter wand adapted to a regular electric Sullivan starter and with a hex socket on its end was inserted up the tailpipe and engaged the hub nut on the impeller. Rotation of the wand was the same as with a regular prop aircraft.

Tractor fans, however, had to be started by hand, which required a deft touch to put enough spin into the impeller. In rare cases, a regular cone starter could be squeezed in front of the fan to engage the spinner. Pod engines were usually the only time this method could be employed.

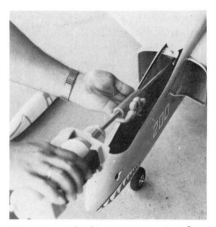

There are only three ways to start fans and this method, the forward probe starter, is the latest, designed by Bob Violett. It consists of a heavy-duty ball hex-head at one end of the probe, a handle to hold it in position, and a spinner at the other end of the probe to engage a standard electric starter. The ball hex-head engages a hex-head bolt in the impeller spinner. Nice feature of this is that the probe can be angled at any offset up to 30 degrees.

Taching a fan is practical since it can help establish reliable operating figures. Yet since impellers are multi-bladed and the tach's logic circuit can read only two or three blades, two strips are usually painted in the spinner hub to fool the tach into reading the impeller as if it were a two-bladed prop.

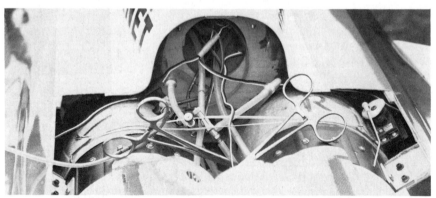

Most modelers clamp their fuel lines to prevent fuel from draining into the engine when it's at rest. If it does drain, a flooded fan engine is a real bear to start. Properly primed, a fan engine starts right away, but if you crank it too long, it will also flood.

Since 1984, two other starter systems have come into being for tractor fans, each designed for a specific intake system. One is Tom Cook's Dynamax starter which uses a Sullivan Dynatron core and a specially designed offset to get the spinner cone into tight places. With a full side intake that has a splitter plate right up to the impeller, this type of starter cannot be used unless there is provision for a removable splitter plate, a technique first used in the Jet Model Products updated Starfire intake system.

The second tractor fan starter system is the Violett starter probe. This is simply a shaft with a ball hex head at one end and a metal cone at the other. On the shaft is a long bushing, usually simple brass tubing. The hex head engages the socket bolt on the spinner and can be angled up to thirty degrees offset. Once the probe is engaged, a regular cone starter is placed over the metal cone while the probe is held by the bushing. The idea is that the probe can be inserted through a small slot in the fuselage as long as there is a straight run to the socket bolt on the impeller spinner. This system also allows a full side intake with an uninterrupted splitter plate.

There is one drawback to this. So far, this will work reliably only if the ball hex head on the end of the probe is at least 1/4 inch. That gives sufficient area to turn the impeller against the compression of the engine without rounding the edges of the ball hex head. A smaller-diameter hex head will round out, especially with prolonged spinning.

It's not a bad idea to create a preflight checklist. Since ducted fans tend to use more complex equipment, they're not simple hop-in-and-go aircraft.

The Byro-Jet was the first to use a starter probe. A long wand with a socket head on it is inserted up the tail-pipe of the jet (like this Byron F-86) and engages the socket head screw on the back of the impeller hub.

147

The radio equipment should be checked not only for correct trim positions but also for correct dual rate or exponential settings. Servo reversing is a blessing, but not when it causes a crash because the setting was changed somehow. Simple, habitual checks can end up saving a lot of money and unnecessary building time.

With the adequate thrust available, the good wing loadings and versatile equipment, flying fans does not take specialized training but there are several characteristics peculiar to them, and the high-performance fans do require familiarity and experience with high-performance aircraft like a pattern plane. These high-performance fans are reaching speeds that were respectable in Formula I pylon racing not so long ago.

The first peculiarity is the takeoff. On a normal single-engine prop plane, the prop wash over the tail control surfaces adds to their normal effectiveness in a clean airstream. This means that the prop wash helps rotate the plane to a climbing attitude more quickly than if the airstream were the simple clean airflow over the surfaces. A fan does not have that advantage. There is no prop wash, so the plane must accelerate to a higher speed before the control surfaces achieve the same effect as the prop plane. The larger air mass moved by a prop as compared to a fan also helps shorten the takeoff roll of a prop plane.

On takeoff, the speed must build. Trying to yank the plane off the ground before it's ready by applying full-up elevator compounds the problem and it actually tends to slow the plane down by adding a lot of drag. If the plane does manage to get into the air, it usually staggers, and control

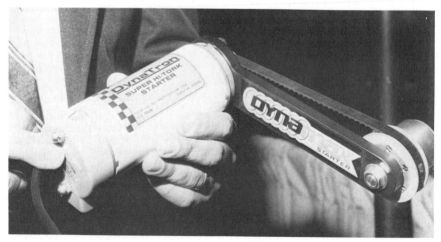

The third method of starting fans relies on this specially made Jet Model Products Dynamax starter. It uses a

Sullivan Dynatron starter coupled to a special offset belt-drive bracket.

surfaces, being less effective at these speeds, give the airplane a wallowing feel. Overcontrol on the sticks results and the usual ending is a crash. Trying to rotate the plane to the unbelievable attitudes seen so often in sport flying is an invitation to trouble. The key in flying a ducted-fan plane is smoothness.

In the air, there's not much difference in flying ducted-fan planes versus prop planes. Roll rates will be generally quick because the wingspans are shorter. Dive speeds need to be managed or they can lead to wing failure. Because the speeds are usually higher than those of a prop plane, pulling out of an inside loop at full throttle can shear a wing. On the down side of a loop, learn to come back on the throttle.

Throttle management is also an important consideration. Just about every fan uses a tuned pipe. These engines have a tendency to richen at idle speeds. Punching the throttle after the engine has been idling for a number of seconds can make it flame out. Up high that's not too much of a problem since the ducted fans generally glide just as well as a prop plane. Down low, as with any plane, it can cause an overshoot. Work with your throttle and learn its characteristic response to different situations. Always apply it evenly, and avoid the panic tendency to jam it when you need power.

Vertical maneuvers need some planning. On a prop plane, when the nose kicks down after a botched vertical maneuver, the prop wash can force the plane to level attitude more quickly than can a fan. It needs some room for recovery so that it can build sufficient flying speed for the surfaces to become effective.

This picture shows the Dynamax starter turning a Dynamax fan unit over.

Landing a jet model is different from landing a prop model. The nose must be kept slightly pitched up during final approach and power used to control the descent rate.

Fan planes are not difficult to land, and many can land at surprisingly slow speeds. The biggest adjustment comes with the fans that have low aspect ratio wings like deltas or some of the newer aircraft. These planforms bleed off airspeed more quickly when they go to a high angle of attack. To establish a good, even approach sink rate, you have to use some power and carefully pitch the nose of the plane up. The glide path is controlled with the power, not the elevator, as is common with most sport flyers. If the power is taken off and the plane dives for the runway, hauling back on the stick to arrest the sink rate when close to the ground pitches the plane up and it slows down. Usually it slows quickly and loses control surface effectiveness.

Some model fans share the same deep stall characteristic as their full-size counterparts. Deep stall simply means that the plane pitches to such a nose high attitude that the tail control surfaces are totally ineffective, yet there is still sufficient lift and forward speed to keep the nose high. The aircraft descends at a rapid rate with the nose high and impacts the ground tail first.

The planforms and the internal arrangements of fan units have presented some unique structural complications for designers of model jet aircraft. The problems they faced and solutions they devised are a good lesson in modeling ingenuity. These solutions offer any jet modeler valuable building techniques, whether you are building a kit or designing your own jet aircraft.

Mike Kulczyk: Saab Viggen, Gloster Meteor and others

Mike Kulczyk has been designing ducted-fan planes since the 1950s. His design process generally starts with a simple, effective technique. He builds a sheet balsa profile glider of the jet which he intends to model and establishes a general center of gravity position with the glider. For planes such as the Saab Viggen with its canard planform, it's quicker than mathematic computation. Once the position has been found, Kulczyk translates the small glider's CG position to the model and moves it forward about five percent to account for the varying weights and three-dimensional property of the fuselage. His reasoning for moving the CG position forward is that a tail-heavy aircraft will always sustain more extensive damage if things have not been figured correctly. With a conservative forward CG the worst that can happen is that the plane will not rotate or will have to be flown with full-up trim or some elevator. A tail-heavy plane pitches too much and is extremely control sensitive.

Kulczyk designed a Gloster Meteor model, Britain's first jet fighter which was used at the end of World War II. This twin-engine fighter presented two structural design problems. The fan units were Axiflo RK-20s, one in each nacelle which interrupt the straight line of the wing spar structure. His problem was designing an adequate carry-through engine nacelle former that would carry the weight of the fan units and outer wing panels and not obstruct the internal duct of the nacelle. Nacelle formers were de-

Mike Kulczyk's AJ37 Viggen relied on the use of a simple balsa profile glider to establish the basic C.G. location, a very important criteria for this unconventional aircraft.

The twin pods on the Gloster Meteor presented Mike Kulczyk with a problem for the spar carry-through structure to amply support the weight of the wings, the fan units in the pods and the aerodynamic loads imposed by flight.

signed with tongues on either side of the circular formers. Each nacelle plugged into a spar wingbox in the center section. Such a spar wingbox was in each of the outer wing panels which then slid onto the outboard tongues of the nacelle. The bulkheads were balsa for lightness and faced front and back with fiberglass. Still, the thin rim of the top and the bottom of the former were a concern for adequate strength. To make this absolutely rigid and strong, Kulczyk first notched the edge of the balsa former all the way around its perimeter and layed in a filament of carbon fiber cord to make it rigid and strong.

Another of the structural considerations Mike encountered was the cruciform horizontal stabilizer on the tail. The term cruciform refers to a horizontal stabilizer which is positioned midway up the vertical stabilizer. This position, and the T-tail position of horizontal stabs, are chosen to keep the stab from being blanketed by the fuselage or wing during a jet's characteristic high angle of attack as it approaches for landing. When a horizontal stab attaches to the fuselage, there is plenty of stiffening structure to keep it rigid and tie the stab's spar to the fuselage. With a tail mounted on a vertical stab, rigidity can be lost if the proper structure is not designed.

To keep the tail strong, he extended the main center spar of the vertical stab down through the top of the fuselage to the bottom and attached it to a small fuselage former at that position. He then attached the main horizon-

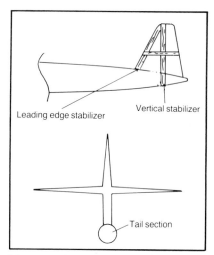

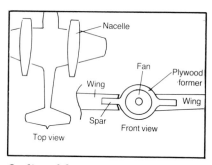

Outline of the spar structure of the Meteor nacelles.

Meteor tail assembly. The tail's leading edge acts as the spar and is tied into the vertical spar. The vertical spar in turn is tied into the fuselage structure.

tal stab spar to the vertical stab spar, and attached the front of the horizontal stab to a second point at the front of the vertical stab's leading edge.

Lynn McCauley: F-84F Thunderstreak, F-104 Starfighter, Stealth

One of the most prolific of the jet designers is Lynn McCauley of Texas who has tackled some difficult subjects and succeeded. Perhaps his best known model is his F-84F Thunderstreak, powered by a Byro-Jet fan which, like Mike Kulczyk's Meteor, used a cruciform tail. On McCauley's F-84F, the tail was a rear swept horizontal stab and it was also an all-flying stab, meaning that the entire surface moved. There are a number of potential structural and aerodynamic problems with this setup, chief among them being flutter. It makes location of the stab pivot point important if the destructive forces of flutter are to be avoided. The sweep of the surfaces presents a structural problem for a spar. Since they are much thinner than a wing, there has to be an adequate method of tying the two stab halves together.

To address flutter, McCauley found a way of balancing the horizontal stab on its pivot point. Because of the narrow chord of the stab, he was almost forced into using the same pivot point location of the full-size airplane, at a point twenty-five percent back on the horizontal stab's chord. Because of the sweep, there was no way of using the traditional method of adding weight forward of the pivot point to balance it like a seesaw. The distance back to the tips of the stab would have meant that a prohibitive weight would have to be added forward of the pivot. The solution was to add a spring attached to a point forward of the pivot, to artificially balance the control surface. Though the stab still drooped at rest, it did not fall straight down.

The cruciform tail on the Meteor presented another structural strength problem to Kulczyk. He solved it by tying the vertical stabilizer spar into the tail structure of the fuselage.

Considered by many as the epitome of jet grace, Lynn McCauley's F-84F Thunderstreak overcame a real problem with the swept, all-moving stabilizer which can be seen here in the drooped position. With so much of the stabilizer's mass behind its C.G. it is an open invitation to flutter. McCauley solved the problem with an ingenious spring-loaded system that allowed the plane to fly quite well.

McCauley's F-104 Starfighter was a design that no one expected to fly, yet it did quite well because of the leading edge flaps and the slight under-cambered wing.

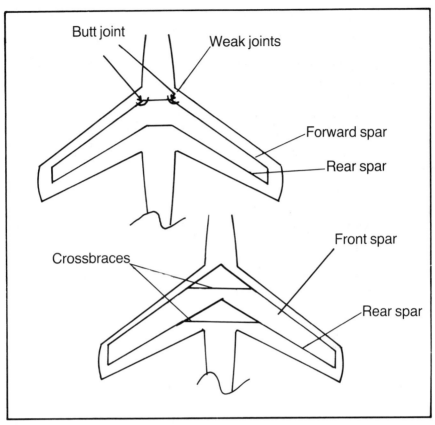

Weak joints on the spar structure, top, lead to wing failure. Crossbracing, bottom, is often required to strengthen the spars, making the wing bracing a much more complex structure.

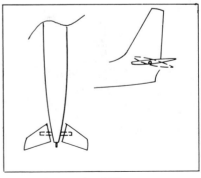

The workings of stabilizers.

The spar structure presented a problem so Lynn devised a way of providing a thin, strong structure. He embedded two nylon bushings in the vertical tail and passed a brass tube through both of them. He then brazed a control horn to the brass rod between the bushings. This control horn attached the spring counterbalance and the stab pushrod. The two stab halves then plugged into the brass tubes.

McCauley usually works with fiberglass and foam as the chief materials in his fuselages and wings, and favors it due to the experimental nature of what he does. Since there is always a high probability of crashing the first example of a new design, the use of a mold and fiberglass fuselage allows several examples of the same plane to be made. To build a wood structure of a complex compound curvature fuselage each time would in the long run be inefficient and time-consuming. McCauley also maintains that using foam wings, especially in swept wings, allows for easier installation of landing gear in a wing.

Many people doubted that McCauley's F-104 Starfighter would fly. The real plane relies on pure power and a minimal wing. It has a very thin wing, designed for speed, not lift. The plane has a T-tail with an all-flying stabilizer, repeating the problem with the F-84F. On the plus side, it could rely on the thrust from the then-new Dynamax fan unit and a full inlet system to improve thrust.

Reducing the model's wings to a scale thickness (the plane was approximately one-eighth scale) would have robbed the necessary lifting capability. So, to preserve scale appearance and provide sufficient lift, McCauley did two things. He increased the wingspan by 1½ inches and undercambered the airfoil like a glider's to get a better lift coefficient. As a further help to lift at low speed, he outfitted the wings with leading-edge flaps coupled to trailing-edge flaps. This last idea worked, but the complexity of the system eventually led to a failure which demolished the plane.

The T-tail of the Starfighter offered the same potential for flutter as the F-84F. To minimize this, McCauley first located the pivot at the aerody-

McCauley's graceful stealth design flew well but suffered from inadequate area of vertical stabilizers. The all- *balsa structure used a Dynamax powerplant.*

namic center of the stabilizer and attached a horn to a point behind the pivot. From this attachment point, the horn ran forward three or four inches parallel to the surface of the horizontal stab. Since flutter is also caused in part by a sloppy pushrod system, McCauley eliminated the long pushrod system by putting the elevator servo in the base of the vertical tail. This gave the pushrod a short run, resulting in a rigid, strong, flutter-resistant actuator.

It should be mentioned here that traditional servo locations in an R/C aircraft are discarded when it comes to ducted fans. There is no traditional radio compartment over or under the wing. The servos, battery and receivers are placed where they offer the best advantage of direct pushrod run to the control surface horn or throttle arm and contribution to proper placement of the CG. The past practice of placing all the radio equipment in one location is no longer necessary and in some cases is impossible and impractical. There are precautions to be taken, especially in long servo cable leads, and the prudent course of action is to protect against possible interference with shielded cables or cables with protection devices inline.

The latest of McCauley's aircraft is a Stealth fighter, a conception of a futuristic fighter design that incorporates the trend toward blended bodies. In a change of technique, Lynn has used balsa wood as the primary material in the plane, as it was easier to make it out of wood than fiberglass based on the profile. For the designer it becomes an intuitive choice, based on a wealth of background experience to evaluate the profiles of an aircraft and determine the most efficient way to construct it. Future jet aircraft will depart from the angular and complex compound shapes of today and assume more functional, squarish outlines. This will benefit wood construction techniques without having to resort to complex substructures.

Rich Uravitch: F-86 Sabre

One of the pioneers of ducted fans is Rich Uravitch. He has experimented with a number of small designs and eventually provided the foundation for a small F-86 Sabre first kitted by House of Balsa and now by Paul's Flying Stuff.

The size of the F-86, built around the small RK-20 Axiflo fan, represents a design philosophy gearing ducted-fan models toward an affordable size and easily constructed model. His choice was based on one significant factor: wing location. Most model propeller designs rely on a one-piece wing attached to the bottom or top of the fuselage. Any other position demands a more complex structure. Present pattern plane designs use plug-in wing tube spars to allow for a mid-wing position on the fuselage but such a structure is not feasible on a jet due to inlet ducting. Consequently, modelers of a mid-wing design have to resort to the tongue-and-wing box method similar to what Mike Kulczyk used on the nacelles of his Gloster Meteor.

Since the F-86 was a low-wing design, the wing became a one-piece structure similar to any sport model. The other factor, used for simplicity and effectiveness, was blow-in doors.

Tom Sewell, Bobby Zieger: BD-40

Blow-in doors act as an internal ramp, directing airflow to the fan, and this ramp effect becomes necessary on designs which do not have the usual jet intake, as is the case with the Jim Bede-designed BD-5J, a small sport jet. The full-size plane uses NASA-style inlets. These inlets, even though they are flush with the surface of the fuselage, direct air to the small jet turbine engine by way of an angled ramp behind the inlet to direct the air to the face of the turbine's first set of blades.

Tom Sewell and Bobby Zieger learned how important this ramp effect could be. After collaborating on a number of successful military scale jet models, they decided to try their hand at designing an everyman's ducted-fan scale model. It would have to be something simple to build with a minimum of internal complexity. Jim Bede's BD-5J became the chosen design.

The inlet was a simple rectangle cut in the side of the canopy-hatch which fed the Turbax I fan inside. This first arrangement did not work well because the air entering the large canopy-hatch chamber became turbulent and slowed down due to the sudden expansion of volume inside. The fan performance suffered and so did thrust.

To restore the thrust loss, they first constructed a simple angled ramp behind the rectangular cutout and aimed the ramp at the front of the fan. The improvement was significant and the plane flew well.

Seeking to boost performance all around for both static and dynamic thrust, they then constructed a full inlet system inside the canopy-hatch which changed the rectangular cutout in the side of the canopy-hatch to a semicircular duct to the front of the Turbax fan. This recent addition to the BD-40 has made the top speed of the plane sparkle.

Here is shown a Uravitch-designed F-86 on takeoff with the side blow-in *doors opened by the full suction of the fan.*

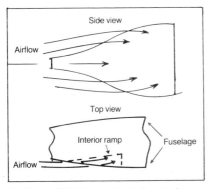

Outline of NASA-style airflow inlets.

Utter simplicity is an elusive goal in fan designs, but the Tom Sewell-Bobby Zeiger collaboration in the little BD-40 has attained it. It did have some teething problems, however. This picture shows the early prototype which had very simple square inlets cut in the sides. They did not allow the fan to breathe properly since both the area and the direction of the inlets worked against the fan.

Incorporating a NASA-style inlet which led to the face of the fan worked a miracle in the performance of the lit- *tle BD-40. It has become a rugged speedster that can operate from grass fields, and is very easy to build.*

Mark Frankel: AJ-5 Vigilante, Gloster Javelin, Lear 35

While the main modern design trend has been to provide smaller airframes with higher thrust for greater speeds, some modelers have experimented with increasing the size of the aircraft and with the use of twin-ducted-fan models. Addressing these complex projects involves new considerations.

Mark Frankel has spent years modeling and researching large twin-ducted-fan aircraft. This choice of subjects and large scale highlight the design factors a fan modeler must consider.

Frankel's use of large airframes parallels design philosophies in the current giant scale propeller movement. Large size adds to the presence of the aircraft and, because of the limited diameters of the fan units currently available, twin-engine aircraft are the only viable choice to achieve sufficient thrust for large airframes.

But there are other positive aspects. Ducted fans experience more vibration at higher frequency levels than model propeller aircraft. Frankel feels that the larger structure can better absorb vibration, is stronger and can generally carry weight better. For example, a small aircraft is penalized with higher wing loadings because of the weight of the fan unit. In critical areas such as takeoff and landing speeds, the numbers must be higher be-

Mark Frankel relied on centerline thrust in his AJ-3 Vigilante design to substantially reduce asymmetric thrust problems should one engine *quit in this twin-engine aircraft. Note the tall vertical stabilizer, necessary to maintain directional stability at high angles of attack.*

cause of the model's weight and the wing area carrying it. Using the same fan unit in a larger aircraft, the wing area increases but the weight of the ducted fan remains the same. Thus, the proportion of powerplant weight carried by the wing diminishes.

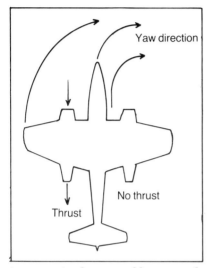

Asymmetric thrust problems can be due to the cutting out of one engine on a twin-engined model.

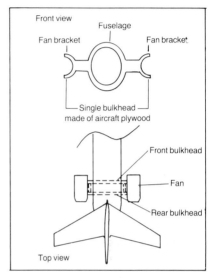

Structure of a podded engine layout.

Mark Frankel's Gloster Javelin also used centerline thrust to alleviate the *asymmetric thrust problem in an engine-out condition.*

161

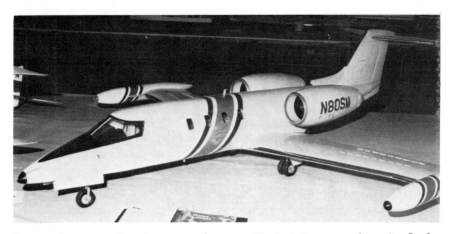

Turning from centerline thrust to podded engines, Mark Frankel came up against the problem of putting two engines and their weight in a position well aft of the center of gravity. It also presented the problem of rigidly mounting the fans so there would not be any flexing.

The primary problem facing David Thompson's Canadair Tutor was the T-tail on the horizontal stabilizer. Positioned at the top of the vertical stabilizer, it had to be rigid enough at the top to maintain the loads imposed by the airflow.

In choosing a twin-engine project, there are other factors to weigh besides the obvious ones of complexity and cost. The first factor is asymmetric thrust, a condition arising when one engine quits on a multi-engine aircraft. The farther away an engine is from the fuselage centerline, the greater its yawing effect should the engine on the other wing quit. If the yaw is not corrected with rudder or by cutting the operating engine, it can lead to a catastrophic spin.

For this reason, Frankel's first two aircraft, the AJ-5 Vigilante and the Gloster Javelin, used centerline thrust. Both engines are placed side-by-side in the fuselage. If one engine quits, the yawing effect is negligible. While centerline thrust is possible in military aircraft where the fuselage can be used to house the engines, it is a problem for transport aircraft which need fuselage space to carry passengers or cargo. To get around this problem, some transport aircraft rely on pod-mounted engines on the rear of the fuselage.

Frankel's latest project, the Lear 35, uses this engine placement which in turn raised several new problems. First, fans far back on an airframe will make the plane tail-heavy. This is the reason Frankel chose the Lear 35; the nose was long enough to counterbalance the added weight in the rear.

Hanging the engines so their mounts are sufficiently strong and rigid becomes another problem, so Frankel used the same method as full-size aircraft. Two large rear bulkheads serve as fuselage formers and also as engine mounts. For the proper strength and rigidity, he used 1/4 inch birch plywood with lightening holes to cut down on weight. Around the engine pods, he placed longerons to lock the two bulkheads in place. Frankel is currently experimenting with the new composite materials for the lightest and strongest bulkhead possible.

He has done most of his prototype work in fiberglass. Though the process is more time-consuming at first, it saves him time in the long run. Since it is rare that the first prototype will have no major bugs to be worked out of it, the mold offers him the ease of creating a second or third fuselage to refine the design to the point of reliability.

David Thompson: Canadair Tutor

New to designing ducted-fan aircraft, David Thompson's Canadair Tutor using a Byro-Jet, shows the adjustments made for scale modeling. After thoroughly researching this Canadian trainer jet, he chose to use the scale airfoil on his model. The Tutor's airfoil used a thick symmetrical section which developed problems in that the real aircraft was subject to pitching with changes in throttle. He found that switching to a semisymmetrical airfoil twelve percent of the original's thickness calmed down the pitching. While not scale, it was a necessary change to translate the real aircraft into a model.

Thompson's wing-mounting method follows the technique adopted by Byron Godberson's Byron Originals method. This method unifies most of the structure through a main wing spar transmitted to a fuselage bulkhead which also mounts the fan unit. This method allows for mid-wing designs and eliminates the need for a large cutout in the fuselage for the wing attachment as is common practice in most R/C models. Large cutouts, especially in a fiberglass fuselage, defeat the purpose of a one-piece structure's strength.

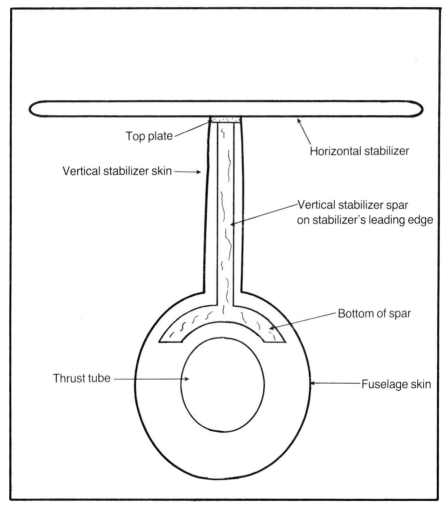

The structure of a high T-tail must be firmly mounted. Here, the rounded *bottom section of the spar ties the vertical stabilizer rigidly into the fuselage.*

Another problem Thompson encountered was the tail structure. The Tutor has a high T-tail so providing a strong vertical stabilizer was necessary. To solve the problem, he used a spar for the vertical stabilizer which tied into the fuselage and the vertical stab as one piece. The curved, or bow, section of the spar matched the curvature of the upper fuselage and did not interfere with the thrust tube. At the same time it gave more surface for the vertical spar's attachment, firmly locking the stab to the fuselage.

Eric Baugher: Performance Phantom

This plane was Eric Baugher's first attempt at designing a ducted-fan plane. Because of his background as a pattern flier, he was more concerned with performance than scale looks and tried to blend both in a single aircraft. Having studied Bob Violett's refinements in ducted fans, he decided to implement the same intake arrangement as Violett had done in a model for a single fan with bifurcated exhaust.

Baugher's design can serve to show the progression of intake design. First, the position of the side intakes and the fan are related to one another so that angle from the inlet to the face of the fan is no more than ten degrees. Second, the total open area of the two inlets matches the swept area of the ducted fan he chose, the Dynamax unit. Third, the inlet remains split right up to the fan face, even enclosing the spinner itself. This last item is the culmination of side intake design first seen on the Bob Violett Sportshark series.

The first arrangement of side intakes for a single fan was simply the inlets supplemented by the cheater hole on the bottom of the fuselage in

Many of the latest design trends have been incorporated in Eric Baugher's Performance Phantom. It uses a bifur- cated thrust tube, a full splitter plate inlet and a starter probe feature.

front of the fan's face. This progressed to a closed Y tube inlet from each intake, although the center was usually just a curve, leaving the two airflows from either side to meet at different angles. This created a turbulent flow in the center of the intake robbing some of the fan's efficiency.

The next step was to separate the two airstreams from either intake until they reached the fan's face, although this splitter plate could only go as far as the spinner. In the short distance from the tip of the spinner to the leading edge of the impeller blades, there would be a gap allowing some of the efficiency gain of the splitter plate to be nullified. Violett's solution was adopted by Eric Baugher in his Performance Phantom; the center section splitter plate was built to also enclose the impeller spinner. That way there could be no efficiency-robbing gap.

Jack Tse's SR-71 has been a design challenge because of the C.G. problem posed by the blended body of the design. The plane must be flown using dual rates, but in an application oppo-site what would be expected. At low speeds, low rate must be selected, instead of the normally anticipated high rate.

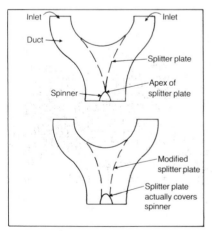

Outline of side inlets and location of splitter plates.

Shown here is the hinge box for the swept wing of Jack Tse's F-14. This spectacular model features a computerized radio to mix the control surface deflections with the variable sweep of the wings. It is the ultimate in ducted-fan model sophistication.

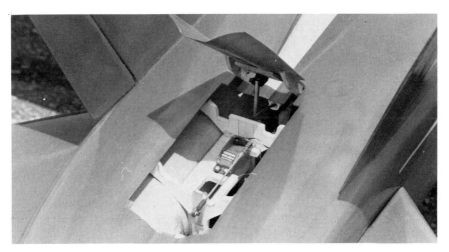

One of the unique features of the Tse F-18 is the operating speed brake at the aft end of the fuselage. It relies on servo actuation.

Baugher's design and that of the latest trend of performance ducted-fan aircraft shows the philosophy of shrinking the airframe down to the smallest size needed to house all the internal components. This reduces wetted area, or the sum total of entire external surface area of the model. Decreasing this wetted area eliminates the drag associated with the simple passage of air over external surfaces, allowing the plane to fly faster.

Jack Tse: various performance aircraft

The work of Jack Tse of Toronto is an example of the complexity that can be designed into ducted-fan models. To date he has engineered some of the most intricate fan aircraft—and gotten them to work. These planes are, by no means, for the average experienced modeler, and in some cases they require two people to successfully fly them.

One aircraft he's flown successfully is an SR-71 Blackbird. Because of the blended body planform and center of pressure range, control throws at various speeds become critical. For example, when first testing the aircraft, Tse found that at low speed, it was sensitive to elevator input. Using the normal throw, the plane would pitch up and stay there. The elevator would become ineffective because the large delta planform was blocking the flow over these control surfaces and the plane could not be pitched down to regain control. At high speed, normal control throws were necessary to fly the plane.

Part of the problem involved the relationship between the center of gravity of the model and the shifting center of pressure. On the real aircraft, the same problem is overcome by a complex plumbing network which shifts fuel to various tanks to change the CG position fore and aft to balance the relationship to the center of pressure. At one point, Tse contemplated using a shifting weight on a sled to do the same thing.

This is Jack Tse's F-18 Hornet design as modeled by Bob Fiorenze. It uses *two Dynamax fans in a very stable airframe.*

His most recent project is a sophisticated F-14 Tomcat. The control surfaces function exactly like the real aircraft and the wings sweep to the scale sixty-eight-degree position. On Tse's F-14, the two horizontal stabilizers function as tailerons, working in conjunction with spoilers mounted on top of the wings for roll control. When the wings reach the fully swept position, the spoilers are turned off and only the tailerons provide roll control. A fully programmed module in a special Profi transmitter radio makes this possible. It is the module, like the onboard computer in the real aircraft, which provides the proper mixing of the control surfaces at the different sweep positions of the wing and which dials out the spoiler actuation in the fully swept position.

While Tse's plane has flown successfully, the proper mixing for attitudes and wing sweep positions still has to be determined. At some pitch attitudes the plane experiences control problems with the wings fully swept so that the wings must be swept forward to regain control. It takes four seconds for the wings to move from one extreme position to the other, and in that time the plane can be lost.

Conclusion

Today, the maturing designs of ducted-fan planes have provided something for everyone. The variety may not be extensive in a specific category but there are simple planes, inexpensive planes, complex planes, scale planes and performance planes—in short, planes for everyone. Some of the more exotic aircraft—and more expensive—are only for the select few. Most of the dissatisfaction and frustration has been with the uninformed selection of an aircraft that is beyond the capability of a modeler. Some of the high-performance aircraft are not for modelers who have not progressed beyond sport aircraft. It's like taking a private pilot who only flies a Cessna 172 and strapping him into the latest jet fighter and telling him to fly it.

The design process has only begun and there are still many problems to address. Noise is one obstacle to ducted fans and has ostracized these planes from many club fields due to noise sensitivity. Work is being done to provide solutions.

The added complexity of working from the inside out is another issue. Modularized designs which take out much of the internal complexity of a ducted fan will extend this facet of modeling to a larger group of people. Seventy percent of the ducted fans available today are not difficult to fly when properly set up.

Cost is another factor and is tied to the complexity issue. The more refined and complex, the greater the cost. The latest ducted fans rely on expensive materials and complex casting and molding procedures when compared with other aspects of modeling. But designers, amateurs though they may be, have always been able to come up with ingenious ways of conquering problems.

Appendix I

Manufacturers and suppliers

ACE R/C
PO Box 511
Higginsville, Missouri 64037
    Among their wide variety of radio systems and accessories, there are several in particular which have direct applications in some ducted-fan aircraft. They are as follows: the Christy Mixer for elevons, the Noise Trap for long servo leads, the 2×5 Redundant Power Supply, and the ACE Digipace for cycling batteries.

Aerospace Composite Products
PO Box 16621
Irvine, California 92714
    Besides fiberglass, this company has an excellent assortment of carbon fiber and Kevlar products in a variety of mats, rods, cloths and sheets suitable for many hobby applications.

Aerotrend Products
31 Nichols St.
Ansonia, Connecticut 06401
    An excellent line of fuel tubing in all sizes, including the thickness of the tubing wall.

Aircraft Spruce & Specialty
Box 424
Fullerton, California 92632
    Although this is a company for full-size homebuilt aircraft, the materials used are almost the same as those used for the composite materials found in model aircraft.

Airtronics
11 Autry
Irvine, California 92718
    This company has a variety of quality radio systems some of which feature the mixing functions and rate adjustments handy for most ducted fans.

Bob Dively Model Aircraft
28001 Chagrin Blvd.
Woodmere, Ohio 44122

Bob Parkinson Flying Models
3 William St.
Thornton, Ontario, Canada LOL 2N0

Bob Violett Models
1373 Citrus Road
Winter Springs, Florida 32708
    Along with K&B Manufacturing, this company produces the specialized KBV .72 engine for use in the Viojett fan. Publishes *The Inlet*. It also produces Magnalite materials, and the Viojett.

Carstens Flying Plans Service
Flying Models magazine
PO Box 700
Newton, New Jersey 07860

Century Jet Models
11B Senior Officer Row
Rantoul, Illinois 61866

Circus Hobbies
3132 South Highland Dr.
Las Vegas, Nevada 89109
The Galaxy and Century radio models in their JR brand offer handy mixing and rate features for fan planes.

Cressline Model Products
635 Third Ave. South
Park Falls, Wisconsin 54552

Fibre Glast Developments
1944 Neva Drive
Dayton, Ohio 45414
All of this company's products are devoted to use of resins and fiberglass. They are a good source, particularly of both epoxy and polyester resins and the accessories used to proportion, mix and apply them. Their catalog contains some concise valuable information about resins, fiberglass repairs and molding procedures.

Futaba
555 West Victoria St.
Compton, California 90220
This company has a quality line of radio systems which include mixing and rate features handy for fan planes. They also produce an electronic accessory called the Tachotimer which is an optical tachometer plus a timer with an aural alarm.

Golden Era Plan Service
Rt. 3, Box 158
Woodland, California 95695
Plans for an AJ-37 Viggen.

High Point Products
3013 Mary Kay Lane
Glenview, Illinois 60025
The primary product of this company is an excellent balancer which can be used to balance spinners, propellers of any kind or impellers for fans. A precision-machined shaft holds the device through its center

hole. Most impellers require the large shaft cone which is available as an accessory.

Hobbico
Great Planes Model Distributing
PO Box 4021
Champaign, Illinois 61820
Distributer of the O.S. Max line of fan engines which include the O.S. .25 VF-DF, the O.S. .46 VR-DF, the O.S. .65 VR-DF, and the O.S. .77 VR-DF.

Hobby Barn
PO Box 17856
Tucson, Arizona 85731

Hobby Lobby International
5614 Franklin Pike Circle
Brentwood, Tennessee 37027

Hobbypoxy
PO Box 378
Rockaway, New Jersey 07866
Along with an excellent line of two-part epoxy paints, this company also has fillers, primers and epoxy adhesives for use with fiberglass or wood components.

JMI Imports
7001 Acton Rd.
Dalzell, South Carolina 29040
Importer of the .80 ci Gleichauf pusher fan.

Jomar Products
2028 Knightsbridge Dr.
Cincinnati, Ohio 45244
One of this company's high-quality electronic accessories can find a valuable application with fan aircraft that need to use long servo lead. The product is their Glitch Buster.

K&B Manufacturing
12152 Woodruff Ave.
Downey, California 90241
Producer of the K&B 3.5 and K&B 7.5 fan engines. The company also

sells a popular polyester finishing resin and a line of two-part epoxy paint.

Kress Jets
4308 Ulster Landing Rd.
Saugerties, New York 12477
Manufacturer of the RK-740 and RK-720 fans.

MACS Products
8020 18th Avenue
Sacramento, California 95826
Tuned pipes for all types of engine are this company's main product. The Wizard pipes are specially designed for ducted fans since they are much shorter than a normal tuned pipe. They come in two sizes, one for .21 ci engines, and one for .45 ci engines.

M. C. Beaulieu Plan Service
84 University St.
Presque Isle, Maine 04769
Plans for an A-10 Thunderbolt.

Model Rectifier Corp.
2500 Woodbridge Ave.
Edison, New Jersey 08817
Importer and servicer of the Rossi line of engines which include the Rossi .65 and the now discontinued Rossi .81 for which parts are still available.

Nick Ziroli Models
29 Edgar Drive
Smithtown, New York 11787
Plans for a small non-scale F-15 and an F-4 Phantom, both of which use a single engine in a bifurcated thrust tube.

Northeast Screen Graphics
21 Fisher Ave.
East Longmeadow, Massachusetts 01028

This company has the widest variety of decals available for most popular sizes of scale aircraft. Besides national insignia, they also have specialized nomenclature decals in pressure-sensitive and water transfer formats. There are three sets of jet nomenclature decals, one for .40 ci jets, one for .60 ci jets and one for the giant-size jets.

Pacer Technology
This company has an extensive line of cyanoacrylate adhesives for almost every application and accessories for these items, which are available through local hobby stores.

Paul's Flying Stuff
PO Box 121
Escondido, California 92025

Penn International Chemical
943 Stierlin Rd.
Mt. View, California 94043
Practically every resin or cyanoacrylate need in modeling applications is covered by the extraordinary variety of resins, cyanoacrylates and accessories produced by this company.

Rhom Products
908 65th St.
Brooklyn, New York 11219
One of the first to produce pneumatic retracts, Rhom has several styles available to fit most applications for aircraft up to fifteen pounds. One model, the #1001 FAI, is a low-profile mechanism that's suitable for thin wings.

Robart
PO Box 1247
St. Charles, Illinois 60174
This company handles many unique, thoughtful products. Their Incidence Meters are invaluable for setting up the proper decalage on an aircraft. They also have some nice scale

landing gear strut accessories. More importantly, they have foam rubber inserts for their line of scale wheels which can firm up a soft tire for a heavy airplane.

Royal Products
790 West Tennessee Ave.
Denver, Colorado 80223

Scale Plans & Photo Service
3209 Madison Ave.
Greensboro, North Carolina 27403
Plans for a large F-4 Phantom (single Byro-Jet) and a large twin-engined Gloster Meteor.

Shamrock Competition Imports
PO Box 26247
New Orleans, Louisiana 70186
This company sells the imported OPS line of engines which includes two fan motors, one in the .80 ci and the other in the .60 ci category.

Sig Manufacturing
401-7 South Front St.
Montezuma, Iowa 50171
This company has a number of resins and finishing products.

Spring Air Products
PO Box 36-1312
Melbourne, Florida 32936

Pneumatic retract systems are this company's product. Their unique feature is a fail-safe down cycle if the system loses pressure. They are spring-loaded to put the gear down. There is also only one air line to the cylinder since pressure is needed only to retract the gear.

Sterner Engineering
661 Moorestown Dr.
Bath, Pennsylvania 18014

Strux Corporation
100 East Montauk Highway
Lindenhurst, New York 11757
For anyone considering the use of architectural foam for making fiberglass plugs, this company is one of the very few that can supply the urethane foam in large billet sizes large enough for the model dimensions. This type of foam can yield the best detail for the model's plug.

Tidewater Engr. & Mach.
PO Box 1135
Bastrop, Louisiana 71220
Importer of the Picco line of engines and is currently distributing the Picco .80 fan engine.

Appendix II

More reading

This brief list can direct you to valuable information if you want to research ducted fans to build one, design your own or simply understand them. These sources were used in providing some of the information in this book and can immensely broaden the scope of your knowledge of this field.

"Aircraft Design Factors for the Midwest RK-20B Ducted Fan" by Rich Uravitch. *Radio Control Modeler,* February 1981, pages 46, 140–150. Using the example of his small F-86 design (now the Paul's Flying Stuff kit), Uravitch describes the problems and solutions of fitting an airframe around this ducted fan unit.

Building and Flying Ducted Fan R/C Aircraft by Dick Sarpolus. Kalmbach Books, 1981, Milwaukee, Wisconsin. ISBN 0-89024-038-8. This is a good overview of early ducted fan kits, operation, and fan units available at the time.

"Ducted Fan Design Principles" by James J. Scozzifavva. *Radio Control Modeler,* June and August 1976. This two-part series is absolute must reading if you are at all serious about ducted fans. It's one of the landmark articles and presents an extremely lucid, comprehensive explanation of ducted fan thrust and its characteristics.

"Ducted Fan Overview" by Mark Frankel. *Model Builder,* July 1985, pages 21–23, 90–91. This is an historical overview of the fan field from the early seventies on.

Ducted Fans for Light Aircraft: Analysis, Design, and Construction by R. W. Hovey. Zenith Aviation Books, 1982, Osceola, Wisconsin. This short book (50 pages) is a brief mathematical look at the theory of ducted fans used for full-size aircraft. The formulas expressed are pertinent to model designs but there is some need to adapt them to the models.

Introducing Model Aero Engines by Mike Billinton. Argus Books, distributed by Zenith Aviation Books, 1983, Osceola, Wisconsin. ISBN 0-85242-804-9. A brief overview of model aircraft engines and explanation of their operation.

"Fan Facts" by Mike Kulczyk. *Flying Models,* a monthly column anchored by Kulczyk every other month with noted fan experts as alternating columnists.

"Jet Blast" by Rich Uravitch. *Model Airplane News,* a monthly column by long-time designer and jet modeler.

Index